Praise for *Different after You* and Michele Neff Hernandez

"Michele Neff Hernandez is an inspiration. She has a true gift for connecting people, giving them hope and camaraderie at a time of profound loss and loneliness. I have been blessed to witness Michele helping hundreds if not thousands of recently widowed people navigate the traumatic landscape of loss with her profound compassion, love, and kindness, giving so many a safe space to heal and connect."

— Marian Fontana, author of *A Widow's Walk*

"Michele not only is committed to providing hope and healing to millions of grievers but has the business acumen and strategic mind to ensure the success of her work for decades to come. Her book, *Different after You*, will fit right into the beautiful, strong world she has created this past decade and take it to the next level."

— Christina Rasmussen, author of *Where Did You Go?* and *Second Firsts*

"*Different after You* serves as a compass for widowed people and those who have experienced any kind of trauma, guiding us on a journey to our true selves. By sharing her personal and professional experiences of grief and trauma, Michele Neff Hernandez has mapped our circuitous path toward self-acceptance and integration. This book is a must-read for all widowed people and anyone whose life has been changed by trauma."

— Amy Yasbeck, actress and founder of the
John Ritter Foundation for Aortic Health

"Michele Neff Hernandez's book, *Different after You*, achieves something that previously seemed impossible: making grief feel less lonely. When I lost my partner Fernando Bengoechea in the 2004 tsunami, and talked about him on *The Oprah Winfrey Show*, many viewers, especially young adults, shared that it was the first time that they had witnessed an expression of LGBTQ grief — and, too, LGBTQ love — in the mass media. After speaking at Camp Widow in early 2020, and now reading Michele's book, I'm reminded of how healing and impactful sharing our pain and experiences can be. *Different after You* addresses almost every question about the grieving process and the individual journey of inhabiting a changed life."

— Nate Berkus, interior designer and author of *The Things That Matter*

"Michele Neff Hernandez is a beacon of light and hope. A generous and soulful visionary, she consistently brings messages of ins   commitment to transforming the lives of widowed p

— Tembi Locke, *New Yor*
From Scratch: A Memoir of L

"Loss changes us in profound and unexpected ways, and we struggle with the stranger within. But thanks to Michele Neff Hernandez and her practical and inspiring book, there's hope. Sharing her own painful loss, Michele comforts and validates our pain as she gently points us through the rubble of grief toward rebuilding a life that better fits our new selves — a life that is different but no less meaningful and satisfying. *Different after You* is a book to read and reread and would make a thoughtful and helpful gift for anyone going through the pain of loss."

— Margaret Brownley, *New York Times* bestselling author of
Grieving God's Way

"I met Michele Neff Hernandez shortly after the death of my wife in 2008. There's no one more connected to, nor anyone who's forged more connections in, the vast and diverse widowed community than Michele. Her commitment to linking people through shared experiences is steadfast, and she's made it her life's mission to build an inclusive network for all widowed people. Sometimes awful things happen and you do your best to make the most of the mess the world has dropped in your lap. Michele has done just that, and helped millions of other widowed people do the exact same thing. Over the years Michele's dream has blossomed in ways that have surprised everyone but her."

— Matt Logelin, *New York Times* bestselling author of *Two Kisses for Maddy*

"For more than a decade, Michele Neff Hernandez has been a leader in the widowed community. Her tireless work has helped shape countless lives and impact them for the better."

— Michelle Steinke-Baumgard, author of *Healthy Healing* and
cofounder of Live the List Nonprofit

"Michele Neff Hernandez took the worst tragedy of her life and, instead of letting it destroy her, turned her pain outward as a light, as a beacon to other widowed people wandering in the same fog. Soaring Spirits has saved lives, including mine, by providing resources and a community that doesn't judge, talk down, or condescend to you. It does not try to fix you or make you the same as you were before your loss, but rather respects and considers the seismic shift in your life and gives you tools to help rebuild."

— Leslie Gray Streeter, author of *Black Widow*

"Michele Neff Hernandez has an uncanny ability to inspire in people a practical, loving, and compassionate belief in themselves and their own ability to heal through the power of community, an ethos she lives by every day. Michele is a natural bringer-together of people and has become a superhero to thousands of grieving people as

she lovingly guides them through the stages of grief, walking alongside them and holding their hand every step of the way."
— Abigail Carter, author of *The Alchemy of Loss* and *Remember the Moon*

"Experiencing the loss of a loved one can be profound, and heartbreaking, and devastating. Michele Neff Hernandez has healed and grown through her own grief to guide so many others from pain to peace, from trauma to triumph."
— Lissa Coffey, author of *Closure and the Law of Relationship*

"For more than a decade, global visionary Michele Neff Hernandez has gracefully and unfailingly stood as brightly as the sun, shining brilliant rays of light onto millions of widowed people living in the dark shadows of grief and trauma. With a profound personal knowing, a passion to create positive change, and a dynamic drive to lead compassionately, Michele founded Soaring Spirits International, the premier peer-based widowed support organization in the world. I am eternally grateful to Michele Neff Hernandez for her ability to help others restore, renew, and rebuild their lives."
— Susan Hannifin-MacNab, MSW, PPSC, author of *A to Z Healing Toolbox*

"Michele Neff Hernandez has the uncanny ability to talk directly to your heart about what it means to experience loss. What makes her especially unique is her unrivaled ability to offer hope and support to those grieving. Spend time in Michele's presence, and you will be changed forever."
— Nancy Saltzman, PhD, author of *Radical Survivor*

"I will never forget the relief I felt in meeting Michele Neff Hernandez just six months into my grief journey. She accepts everyone where they are and welcomes them into her community. Her amazing ability to connect with people, whoever they are and whatever their background, made me feel at home. It has been a blessing and an inspiration to know and learn from her."
— Harold S. Buchanan, chairman of Helping Other People Evolve, Inc., and coauthor of *Seven Sisters and a Brother*

"Michele Neff Hernandez is an innovator. Through her work founding Soaring Spirits International, Michele has repaired many wings and inspired thousands of widowed people to know, love, and celebrate the people they are today."
— Dr. Gloria Horsley and Dr. Heidi Horsley, authors of *Open to Hope* and founders of Open to Hope

"Born with the longest arms, Michele Neff Hernandez can wrap them around thousands of people at once through her words of comfort, care, and concern.

She has lifted thousands of people from great pain to personal empowerment through her insightful programs and her gentle touch of everyday thoughts, shared through her presentations. In true honesty, she is a 'widow whisperer,' one who provides people with tools to learn, live, and love themselves in order to be the best versions of themselves."
— Rachel Kodanaz, bestselling author of
Living with Loss, One Day at a Time and *Finding Peace, One Piece at a Time*

"In her writing, in her organizing, in her speaking, and in her companionship, Michele Neff Hernandez changes lives. What a gift for those of us who have lost our beloved partners."
— David Hallman, author of *August Farewell*

"Michele Neff Hernandez did not let her own story of loss and grief defeat her. Instead, she turned it around to help others. I have never seen anyone so tireless in her mission. She is visionary. She is unstoppable. I have profound admiration and respect for this woman who lives and breathes to help widowed people heal."
— Amy Florian, author and founder of Corgenius

"Michele Neff Hernandez excels at connecting with her audience while gently challenging them to stretch out of their comfort zone. She believes fundamentally in honoring loss and in helping people find meaning and joy in the wake of it. She challenges us to expand our view, plant seeds that grow over time, and allow ourselves to find our own insight and healing."
— Jenny Woodall, grief specialist, National Fallen Firefighters Foundation

"Michele Neff Hernandez has an incredible gift of truly connecting, on a heart and soul level, with the thousands of widows she serves through Soaring Spirits International. Her hard-earned wisdom and empathy are a comfort to anyone who is dealing with the excruciating pain after losing a life partner. She is an inspiring hero, and through her example of living her best life after loss, she shows that it is possible to rise and thrive in widowhood."
— Tanya Villanueva Tepper, 9/11 widow featured in the
Peabody Award–winning film *Rebirth*

DIFFERENT
AFTER
YOU

DIFFERENT AFTER YOU

Rediscovering
Yourself and Healing
after Grief and Trauma

Michele Neff Hernandez

FOREWORD BY Kristine Carlson

New World Library
Novato, California

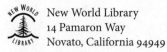

New World Library
14 Pamaron Way
Novato, California 94949

Text design by Tona Pearce Myers

Library of Congress Cataloging-in-Publication Data

Names: Hernandez, Michele Neff, author.
Title: Different after you : rediscovering yourself and healing after grief and
    trauma / Michele Neff Hernandez.
Description: Novato, California : New World Library, [2022] | Summary:
    "Empowers people who have experienced a life-altering trauma to grieve
    what they've lost, identify what they've gained, and embrace the person
    they've become through the process"-- Provided by publisher.
Identifiers: LCCN 2021049905 (print) | LCCN 2021049906 (ebook) |
    ISBN 9781608687787 (trade paperback) | ISBN 9781608687794 (epub)
Subjects: LCSH: Self-actualization (Psychology) | Loss (Psychology) |
    Grief--Psychological aspects. | Identity (Psychology)
Classification: LCC BF637.S4 H484 2022 (print) | LCC BF637.S4 (ebook) |
    DDC 155.9/3--dc23/eng/20211119
LC record available at https://lccn.loc.gov/2021049905
LC ebook record available at https://lccn.loc.gov/2021049906

First printing, February 2022
ISBN 978-1-60868-778-7
Ebook ISBN 978-1-60868-779-4
Printed in the USA on 100% postconsumer-waste recycled paper

New World Library is proud to be a Gold Certified Environmentally Responsible Publisher. Publisher certification awarded by Green Press Initiative.

10   9   8   7   6   5   4   3   2   1

Dedicated with gratitude to Dan Neff.
I love you, Papa.

Contents

Foreword

I first heard of Michele Neff Hernandez and her organization Soaring Spirits in 2010 when my book *Heartbroken Open* came out. At that time, I felt quite alone being a younger widow, and I was relieved to know there were more of us out there. Ten years later, Michele and I met in person for the first time as she had invited me to be her keynote speaker for an upcoming Camp Widow.

As I stood in front of 350 grieving people, I realized that this was a massive club nearly all of us take membership in at different times — grieving the loss of a life partner. A club no one wants to be a part of. If you have become a member of this unpopular club, too, those of us who welcome you do so with a deep understanding that comes from experience. We know how you are suffering during this unimaginable time of change. It's truly one of the highest pain vortexes we reach as earthly beings, detaching from our life partners as they find their wings, and we are left behind — to learn how to let go, to live more and love again. And that's not an easy process.

Or maybe what brings you to this book is another kind of pain — another kind of cataclysmic change. Your world shifted in some way that you probably weren't prepared for. It may be a serious illness, a divorce, an accident, the death of a close friend, or the end of something you have loved dearly, such as a career or a longtime home. In some inexorable way, the proverbial rug has been pulled out from under you, and you're looking for solid ground.

There was a time when I, too, had the rug pulled out from under my feet. My late husband, Dr. Richard Carlson, died suddenly from a pulmonary embolism while on a flight to New York City — as far east from California, from me and our daughters, as he could be without traveling to another country. A happiness guru for the world, my beloved just vanished into thin air. I died with him that day as my life unraveled and my heart shattered from heartbreak. I joined the club that day and have been a member ever since.

There's no one who understands what it feels like to live with grief except those who have walked the path before you. Only they can hold out their hand and say to you, "I'm here; you don't have to walk alone. I will help you learn how to step forward and step into this new life where you are different now. Different because you've loved."

Michele is a woman who found purpose and meaning in her loss. She is the triumphant warrior we all wish to be. She is a hero for many souls who are grasping for a lifeline to pull them out of the trenches of sorrow. It's true that spirits soar — and we are left behind to live some more. Michele shows us how to do what at first seems impossible.

Different after You is the book that shows the way and will inspire its readers on so many levels. Michele points to one of the most undeniable feelings we all have during loss or another kind of unwelcomed change: wishing our lives would go back to what they were *before* — when our loved one was alive or before the traumatic event took place. We ache for and are attached to the life we had, and moving forward somehow means moving on. But it really doesn't. Moving forward means *living*.

This heartfelt book will inspire you to live, not by denying your past but instead by integrating your past with the present as you create your future by stepping in. You'll find solace as Michele shares her own powerful journey through loss. You will laugh with her and cry with her as you see your own story in hers. *Different after You* acknowledges your loss but will help you choose to move forward into your new life as you mend your broken heart.

You are different because you have loved. You have loved people and places and the many gifts that life has given you. It is worth it to love greatly even though it is difficult to let go. Yes, it's incredibly hard to let go, but life gets easier as you let go.

This book is a gift beyond measure to all its readers as we receive the blessing of Michele Neff Hernandez and her profound desire and willingness to serve humanity. She shows us that our spirits can also soar in this life, as our loves are never truly lost to us.

Treasure the gifts of life and love,
Kristine Carlson,
coauthor of the *New York Times* bestselling
Don't Sweat the Small Stuff series

Introduction

Trauma changed me. The person I became after the death of my husband Phillip in a cycling accident was unfamiliar — her needs foreign and the way her brain worked unfathomable. Phillip's death left me grieving not only him, but me. When our life is altered by any kind of irreversible circumstance, we wake up the next day in a new, and often unwanted, world.

If you have experienced emotional damage due to grief or trauma and believe this has made you a lesser version of yourself, I've written this book for you. *Different after You* offers solace, understanding, and a path forward for anyone who has been changed in the wake of a traumatic experience and finds themselves struggling to return to the person they were before.

In these pages, I encourage you to name, explore, and own the trauma that has changed you. Perhaps you are grieving the death of a loved one or of the life you once lived. Perhaps you have survived a tragic event or illness, and the aftermath of that experience continues to reverberate in painful ways. Each person's experience is unique, but what's common to all is the work of rediscovery in the aftermath of tragedy. The premise of this book is that these types of transformative events change us, making it impossible to return to the self that existed before tragedy walked into our lives. Instead, I want to help you find, accept, and celebrate the version of you that has lived through a life-altering event. This new you is unique and valuable. The purpose of this book is to help you claim and embody the changes that have created this person.

Different after You offers a path through the wilderness of self-doubt and self-loathing that so often accompanies grief and trauma, and it leads you toward an acceptance and understanding of the you born through tragedy. Throughout, I share my personal and professional experiences to show that you are not alone in this work. I have lived through this process and personally embraced these themes and methods, and I have also worked with thousands of other people to help them identify their new selves in the wake of grief and trauma.

After nearly two decades of working with the widowed community, I've met many survivors who have outlived a partner and are trying to find the will and the inspiration to create a new life for themselves. Others have experienced the death of a person with whom they shared a different pivotal relationship — a child, a sibling, a parent, or a friend. Even though circumstances differ, all struggle to reimagine their lives without that beloved person's physical presence. I've also met people who have suffered through critical illnesses of the mind and body, as well as traumatic experiences of all kinds, and their stories, struggles, and triumphs are all reflected in these pages. This process of rediscovery is designed to assist anyone whose heart has been broken by death, trauma, illness, or tragedy, to embrace the person they are becoming as they heal.

How to Use This Book

The process of grief and healing is not linear. We each recover and rediscover ourselves in our own ways and at our own pace. Keep this in mind as you read this book. While I have organized the book in a step-by-step way — beginning with acknowledging and grieving what happened and proceeding through taking inventory, exploring possibilities, imagining a new future, and then reclaiming and owning one's new self — that may not be how you go through or experience the process in your life. All the steps in the process are important and work in concert together, and the book is written so that each step prepares you for the next. But take each step at your own pace and follow your own path.

Different after You is not intended to be consumed all at once. Allow yourself to be immersed in each section until you feel ready to move to the next. If any themes or questions feel challenging or hard to accept, sit with them. Wrestling with these ideas is a crucial part of the discovery process, which is designed to help you look at trauma's influence on your identity and sense of self through a new lens. Before moving to a new section, check in with yourself to see how what you've just read has settled with you. Give yourself permission to stop reading whenever you want, especially if a message resonates strongly with your experience. Let the words sink slowly into your mind, your heart, and your soul.

In chapters 1 and 2, I introduce the key concept of integration. This is the simple idea that everything we experience — in our past, right now in the present, and what we anticipate in the future — impacts us, how we see ourselves, and what choices we make. This concept changed my life and informs the entire process. However, I encourage you to reflect on and incorporate these lessons in the ways that speak to you and to make this book your own. While reading *Different after You*, please write in the margins, fold the pages, spill coffee on the cover. Nothing would make me prouder than for this book to become a dog-eared volume with many of your own words written in the margins. Then again, reading the book won't be enough. In order to change your life, you must be willing and ready to make the effort each step requires.

Ultimately, *Different after You* offers an opportunity to learn how to celebrate a new version of yourself, and it encourages you to walk around in your new skin with pride.

As you read, I also suggest being honest with yourself about whether you are emotionally ready for this work. If someone's tragic experience happened very recently, they might find it's too soon to start or finish the process in this book. If someone is just beginning to walk through the changes that a tragedy has caused, they might need to give their full attention to their pain and emotional damage. This is a normal part of healing. Always ask yourself if you have the mental, emotional, and physical energy to explore these ideas about rebuilding your sense of self. Give yourself some grace if the answer is no. If now is not the time for personal rediscovery, put *Different after You* on a shelf in a place where you can see it. When the time is right, this work will still be waiting.

Surround Yourself with Support

Another thing to keep in mind is that *Different after You* is not meant to be your only resource for processing pain and healing from trauma in order to build a new life. Use this book along with every other resource that resonates with you for trauma recovery and integrating your life-altering experiences. To fully rediscover yourself, seek out every form of support possible, including individual therapy, support groups, peer networks, workshops, books, blogs, articles, TED Talks, You-Tube clips ... and anything else that helps you discover the new you, day by day.

Learning to know and love ourselves is a lifelong experience in the best of circumstances. When trauma is a part of our story, the learning curve steepens and flexibility is required. We may have to revisit certain steps in the recovery process many times, and new challenges may confront us and present obstacles that slow or interrupt our efforts. My hope is that the tools offered within these pages will help you to develop skills and coping techniques that will serve you for the rest of your life.

Different after You is meant to be a book you return to when your heart hurts — a source of reassurance and understanding when the winds of grief are stirred or when a past experience casts a shadow on your future. The work of rediscovery is messy. My sincere hope is that *Different after You* will become a good friend and companion as you walk the road ahead.

One thing I know for sure is that there is great potential in the new version of you. I promise that *Different after You* will help you celebrate every iteration of you that emerges from any experience that changes your life.

Chapter 1

Begin Here

People who have lived through a traumatic experience are often encouraged to behave as if the trauma that changed their lives did not happen. Pretending that our past is not an influential part of our life is both difficult and harmful. Instead, whenever we endure an excruciating ordeal, our work is to treat the experience as part of a whole.

After the death of my husband Phil, I felt pressured to quickly turn my focus from grief to life. I was quietly encouraged by people witnessing my grief to skip over the sad part and move into creating a new happy life for myself — but I couldn't. When my husband lost his life, I also lost mine. That fact couldn't be ignored or wished away. Grieving was work that the new me had to do.

In the immediate aftermath of a traumatic experience, triage is usually the first step. Assigning degrees of urgency to our needs and dealing with them in order of critical importance requires focused energy. This is crisis mode, which can be overwhelming, since we must make decisions and manage our most pressing needs first in order to get through the crisis.

The first days of dealing with Phil's death included unknown experiences for me, like planning a funeral and determining how to donate my husband's organs. There wasn't time to think about what I was doing; the tasks had to be completed immediately. The time-sensitive needs associated with managing the early days of trauma can be urgent and intense, but the intensity is often finite. Once the critical demands of the moment have been met, the work of living with our new reality begins.

This effort is less frenzied, but the wounds we must now address are deep and layered. Catastrophic experiences often leave us remembering and yearning for the life we lived before, but that is no longer possible. Our work is to integrate the life-altering experiences we've had while building a different life that acknowledges our wounds and our pain. This process may not feel natural at first. When Phil died, I was not interested in developing a new life. I wanted my old one back, desperately. I spent a lot of time longing to return to the life that was just out of my reach. This is a normal part of healing.

For instance, one afternoon while sitting in the waiting room at the dentist's office, I heard a receptionist say to her coworker, "Phil should be here in a few minutes to look at the air-conditioning unit."

At the mention of the name *Phil*, my heart began to pound and my palms started to sweat. My Phil was also an HVAC tech and had been about to start his own business. I sat in stunned silence as tears rolled down my cheeks, the words on the page of the magazine blurred, and I repeated to myself over and over: *Phil is dead. Phil is dead. Phil is dead.*

Then I heard voices right outside the door. Straining to catch a word or two of the conversation, I could not sit still any longer. I walked quickly into the other room and straight into a man who was not my Phil.

I knew it couldn't be him, but the disappointment was still crushing.

When we are grieving a person we love, a sense of disbelief regarding their death can surface repeatedly, even if we witnessed their death. Our minds and our hearts ache for a sense of security and a return to a life where the person we love is alive. We can't help thinking that perhaps they really are fixing the air-conditioning system at the dentist's office or driving the car just three vehicles ahead.

This sometimes-desperate craving for a different outcome to our situation often pulls us toward the past, particularly when we grieve a death. Knowing that going back in time is impossible, we might fight against our yearning to return to the past. We know we cannot re-create or relive the time before tragedy appeared. However, focusing primarily on leaving behind the pain of the past and moving into a better future can diminish our experience — including the values we've learned, the coping strategies that helped us survive, and the powerful confidence that comes from having lived through something awful.

No matter what type of trauma someone experiences, this desire to return to, or even to create, a time of safety and certainty is common. The hunger for a past version of life can take many forms. Some people might daydream of a life where they never met the person who harmed them. They might dream they took a different path home or chose not to get into a car. Someone might imagine a life in which they or someone they love never contracted a life-altering illness. They might imagine a different outcome for a loved one who struggled with addiction.

On the other hand, some people find they are propelled away from the past. They want to avoid "giving air to" or "being held back by" the challenges they have endured. People frequently advise taking this approach in regard to traumatic events. They treat the past as something to overcome, and believe that revisiting tragedy and harm will give these painful experiences undue power over our future. They try to leave any pain "in the rearview mirror."

Trying to forget what happened can be terribly tempting and even seem momentarily possible. The trouble is, ignoring pain does not remove the trauma. We may wish desperately to just walk away from the painful parts of our past and simply wake up in a new life, refreshed and free of heartache. But we need to understand our past to make sense of our reactions, fears, and even strengths in the present. We need access to every part of our lived experience to truly know ourselves and to develop the tools and resources that will help us cope better in the future. Without acknowledging where we have been, we cannot understand how we got to the place we are in today or know what we want for tomorrow. Otherwise, it's like we are living within a one-dimensional world. Focusing only on the present moment might provide a momentary escape from a painful past or an uncertain future, but it won't provide lasting relief. The same is true if we try to avoid a painful present by daydreaming of a far-off future or remembering fondly a happier past. The desire to escape emotional pain is normal, and even valuable. Yet despite the fleeting comfort this type of avoidance provides, everything is connected. The past affects the present, which influences the future, and we cannot separate one time perspective from another.

This concept of the interconnectedness of past, present, and future is called integration — the blending of all our experiences into a single whole. This simple idea provides a life-changing lens of perception that can be used as a dynamic healing tool for mending our hearts and living a full and meaningful life. In my experience — in my life, my research, and my work with others, particularly related to widowhood — I've found integration to be the foundation upon which transformation happens.

In our daily lives, we constantly toggle between the three perspectives of past, present, and future, sometimes at rapid speed. When we process trauma, we can facilitate healing by developing an awareness of how the three perspectives are connected and an appreciation of the influence they have on one another, rather than viewing each perspective individually. The concept of integration encourages us to consider all three as valuable parts of a whole, and by balancing our attention among them, we can improve our sense of self, our relationships, and our future.

Chapter 2

The Three-Legged Stool

In 2005, when Phil died, I was thirty-five years old with three children under the age of fifteen and three stepchildren aged seventeen, nineteen, and twenty-one. Every part of my experience was foreign, and though I knew I could not possibly be the only widow in the world, I felt completely alone. Not knowing where to turn to ask questions about managing this new life, I sought out other widowed people in the hopes that they knew more than I did. Eventually, through a variety of personal connections, I sat down for a good long talk with thirty different widows who were willing to share their stories with me. During the course of hours of interviews, we talked, we cried, we laughed, and we frequently completed each other's sentences. The understanding I found with these strangers with whom I shared the widowed experience made surviving my husband's death feel possible.

The first year after Phil's death, speaking with other widowed people inspired feelings of normalcy and hopefulness in a way that nothing else did. After every one of these conversations, I left with the wish that anyone who outlived a partner could experience the relief that comes from sharing their broken heart with someone whose heart has been broken in a similar way. These thirty life-affirming conversations inspired me to create a space for widowed people to connect, feel understood, and begin to believe in a positive future for themselves and their families. The desire to connect widowed people with one another, to research the impacts of widowhood, and to develop methods for fostering resilience became my calling, one that eventually shaped my personal tragedy into a force for good.

I didn't know anything about research or nonprofit work when I started. However, in 2008, in order to foster the same kinds of conversations I was having and to help other widowed people rebuild their lives, I imagined the retreat and workshop now called Camp Widow. That same year, I founded Soaring Spirits International, a nonprofit organization, for the purpose of providing resources and programs that would reach even more people grieving the death of a spouse or partner (for more, see "About Soaring Spirits International," page 191). Through this outreach and direct experience helping people in all types of circumstances, I discovered an enduring truth: We are changed by surviving significant traumas, and in order to adapt to our lives after trauma, we must navigate new ground, solve new problems, and develop new coping skills.

Further, through our research at Soaring Spirits, we discovered that a key element for building resilience after tragedy, particularly widowhood, is the concept of integration, or acknowledging all of our experiences and seeing how our past impacts our present and how our present shapes our future.

Let's look closer.

To see integration at work, consider any everyday event or activity, like mowing the lawn. Whatever we are doing in the present, our decisions are influenced by both our past experience and our expectations or plans for the future. While mowing the lawn, we are simultaneously remembering what we've done in the past — such as how to use a lawn mower or the location of rocks to avoid, and so on — and considering the future: perhaps how satisfied we'll feel to have a trim lawn or how we might avoid ever mowing the lawn again. Literally every life experience is lived in this way, including the traumatic events that cause fundamental shifts in our sense of self.

Consider something more serious, like physical trauma. If someone were to fall and break an ankle, they would immediately experience pain, inconvenience, and alterations in daily functioning. But their past experience and their expectations for the future would influence how they met those challenges in the present, and this might impact how quickly and how well they heal. If as a child their mother suffered from diminished mobility, and this made her miserable and emotionally unavailable, this might increase the person's anxiety because their past experience tells them to expect to suffer in ways that impair their relationships with the people they love. Our past experiences live in the cells of our bodies, and they influence and inform the way we process every life situation.

Further, if these expectations make the person's recovery from a broken ankle stressful and difficult, they might come to associate physical injury with emotional trauma, and they might approach any future injury with a higher level of anxiety. Today's lived experience is imprinting itself on our memory and shaping our expectations of the future. Then again, if healing from a broken ankle led to an enjoyable month of bingeing great TV shows and being catered to by caring people, someone might approach a future physical injury with less trepidation and a long list of shows to watch! A positive experience also affects our future expectations.

Our past, present, and future are irrevocably connected. As we make our way through our daily lives, we count on the continuity between past, present, and future to provide a frame of reference for daily decisions, large and small. Access to resources and experiences from our past shape the decisions we make, the quality of the relationships we have, and the way we process and acclimate to every life experience. We are constantly processing the past and creating the future while living in the present. This cyclical pattern shapes and reshapes our lived experience to provide our minds and hearts with ever-changing information about the world around us.

Despite the interconnectedness of these time perspectives, many people can still think of them as separate and value one perspective over another. For instance, advertising and marketing campaigns, music and literature, and pop culture in general often promote the message that the past is the past, and it should be left behind or forgotten in order to shape a positive future. The problem is that acting as if something horrible did not happen does not change the reality that it happened. We cannot truly separate ourselves or walk away from our past experiences. Trying to do so only distances us from ourselves and from the lessons we have learned, robbing us of the power and confidence that come from surviving something awful. Cutting ourselves off from our past does a disservice to our well-being.

The same is true when people say we should live only in the present. This idea reflects the principles of the mindfulness movement. Having outlived my husband, I walk through life with a deep understanding that this moment is the only one we are guaranteed — and that vivid reality influences my daily perspective. An understanding of the finite nature of life and the power of now is important. But I've come to realize there's more to "now" than meets the eye. Since Phillip's death, I no longer perceive the present moment as a segment of time that exists as a kind of protective zone, a spiritually sanctified bubble of sorts. I know in my bones that the present is inextricably connected to the past and the future, no matter how much we talk about them as separate cycles.

Another way people sometimes try to separate these time perspectives is to regard the future as a blank page, one we can fill in any way we want. We should dream big and not allow the past to determine our future, and we should start building that future now, urgently. We don't have time to wait. This one-dimensional view of the future discounts the fact that all of our lived experience is stored in our bodies, our hearts, and our minds. In every moment, the present is constantly becoming the past, which continually informs and shapes the next moment and the next. There is no way to begin with a blank slate; we must create our future by building from what already exists.

Another way to visualize the concept of integration is as a three-legged stool. Each time perspective is one leg, and each is necessary to keep the stool balanced and stable. Remove a leg, and the imbalance will cause a person to fall unless they compensate to hold themselves up. Adjusting to that sense of lopsidedness and insecurity can be done; in fact, humans are generally excellent adapters. However, it takes work and energy and constant attention not to fall over, since a two-legged stool can't hold someone up on its own. Like a three-legged stool, all three time perspectives need to be kept in mind for us to feel balanced and stable.

These ideas reflect what's called the "time perspective theory," which was developed by a team of pioneering researchers, Philip Zimbardo, Rosemary Sword, and Richard Sword. In essence, by integrating and balancing our past, present, and future time perspectives, we can change negative coping techniques. This approach has been used in both clinical and personal evolution settings, such as workshops, training programs, and life coaching work, and it has helped people experience improved self-worth and develop healthy coping strategies for facing life's challenges. A form of cognitive behavioral therapy, it has been particularly valuable as a means for processing and moving through traumatic life experiences.

When we focus our energy on integrating the lessons learned in the past with the immediacy of our present experiences, we can use what we learn to craft a future that reflects our whole selves. This integration allows us access to a huge database of information amassed throughout our lifetime rather than attempting to segregate the time perspectives from one another.

Instead of cutting out our past as a way to remove the pain we've lived through, we integrate that past with our present to process the trauma, and then use that experience as a tool in the future.

Instead of isolating the present as the only moment that counts, we take the tools developed in the past and use them to handle current experiences, which then develop into knowledge and perspective for the future.

Rather than dream of a future not impacted by the past, we find ways in the present to shape our future, counting on the lessons of the past for guidance. Integration allows us to blend what was with what is and what will be, providing the necessary stability for fostering healing.

That said, in any particular moment, one time perspective might dominate. If the present is painful and the future uncertain, we might naturally focus on remembering the past as a safe retreat. If our present is very busy — because we are raising children, caring for elderly parents, or launching a new career — then our focus might be only on the present. If we are planning a big event, organizing the trip of a lifetime, or awaiting the birth of a new family member, the future may constantly occupy our thoughts. A temporary focus on a singular time perspective is a natural part of the ebb and flow of life.

The power of the concept of integration lies in our ability to value each time perspective individually while recognizing their impact on one another and on our sense of self. By developing this new relationship with past, present, and future, we transform the concept of integration into a living and breathing healing force. Access to this powerful source of healing is particularly valuable as we make our way through difficult life experiences. We need the respite and the frame of reference offered by every area of our life in order to access the unique, individual tools available within for healing and renewal.

Even when we are hyper-focused on one particular segment of our lives — past, present, or future — there is no escaping the fact that each time perspective influences the others. We learn things from past experiences that influence our present and shape our future. When Phil died, I learned that I could live through the death of an instrumental person in my life. That confidence, though developed in one of the worst ways, is something I count on every day. My present is lived with the benefit of certainty that I can survive hard things. My future is being built upon a foundation created by that knowledge. Developing my own integration practice has fostered healing through my grief experience and provided me with tools and resources that I use to manage everyday life — and upon which I know I can rely as my future unfolds.

I've come to understand that every person can benefit from a daily practice of integration, and that for those suffering from a trauma, integration is often the key to processing a life-altering experience. My hope is that the work in this book will help you to identify the realities, lessons, and influences unique to your past, present, and future. As you view your world through this holistic lens, you will develop the ability to integrate any life-altering experience into your life. Hope, courage, and confidence are built when we access every lesson learned from surviving trauma.

These skills add value to our lives on a daily basis. Even when we'd rather have learned these lessons in another way. Even when we've acquired these skills through events that broke our hearts. The fact remains; if we can integrate the changes that painful experiences have caused, we will be more content, more resilient, and happier as a result.

Let's begin together.

ACKNOWLEDGE

You Have Been Changed

⊰——⊱

The death of someone or something we love changes us. There is no going back to the person we were before this life-altering experience. We will never be that version of ourselves again. No amount of effort or reflection or mental gymnastics will return us to our pre-tragedy self.

Chapter 3

What Came Before

Phillip Hernandez and I met on a high school track; he was fast, and I was in the way.

My daughter, Caitlin, was eight, and she finally felt ready to join the track team that one of her friends ran with regularly. I had signed on to be an assistant coach for the youngest group of girls, who were warmly referred to as the Gremlin Girls. Phil was coaching the youth boys, who were the oldest and fastest group on the track.

The community track club for which Phil and I volunteered was a large, well-run organization. As one of the newest coaches, I met the other club volunteers whenever our paths crossed, but each age group was an individually functioning part of the larger team. One afternoon while I was jogging on the track with my group of five- to eight-year-old girls, Phil went whizzing past me in the lane right next to us. He looked like a very tan version of a Greek god who was being chased by a pack of long-legged teenage boys. Hurriedly, I gathered the girls together so that they wouldn't be trampled by the flying stampede. As Phil ran by, he yelled, "Track!" This was my signal to let the faster runners pass. My first impression of him was a blur, a shout, and the distinct feeling that the kids and I had narrowly avoided disaster. Shaking my head as I checked to be sure all my little girls were accounted for, I mentally categorized him as arrogant and promptly forgot he existed.

Over the course of that track season our paths crossed now and again, but I spent most of my time ensuring that none of my girls were run over by his boys. Despite my tendency to avoid him that spring, Phil seemed to pop up around every turn. He was definitely a superstar on the track. Popular among the other coaches, and never without his signature smile — Phil was hard to miss.

That same year, in December 1999, I was hired to manage a local fitness center. In an effort to become familiar with our facility, for my first month I scheduled myself to work every shift during our open hours. Arriving for work at four in the morning, I was surprised to see Phil on the weight-room floor. It was the off-season for track, and I wasn't sure he would recognize me, but as a fellow coach I was expecting a friendly conversation and went over to say hello. He only managed about ten words before telling me that he needed to get on with his workout. A little insulted and totally annoyed, I walked back to my office and wondered why he was so popular on the track.

Since I taught fitness classes and offered personal training at the gym in addition to my managerial responsibilities, I often started and ended my day in workout gear. On New Year's Eve, I didn't have any classes or clients, so I put on my favorite outfit and enjoyed not wearing a ponytail and spandex to work for a change. Dropping the kids off at the on-site day care, I was feeling confident and professional as I headed to my office down the hall. Turning the corner, I ran directly, and literally, into Phil. As we backed away from each other, I greeted him and asked how he was. He just stared at me. Standing right in front of me, he didn't even say hello. Confused by his curt behavior, I walked into my office, shaking my head yet again at this man who somehow endeared people to him despite his regularly rude behavior.

An hour later, the front desk clerk came in to tell me Phil Hernandez was on the phone for me. "What does he want?" I asked. "He just asked for you," he replied. I quickly pulled up Phil's account on my computer just to be sure there weren't any unresolved membership issues, then I took a deep breath and answered the phone. I almost fell out of my chair when he asked me if I would have lunch with him sometime. Stunned by his sudden interest, I stammered a bit as I told him that I didn't know when I would be available. He told me to give him a call anytime, and we would work something out. Hanging up the phone, I wasn't sure if I would ever call him back — but recalling his mischievous smile, I knew that I was intrigued by his offer.

Two weeks later, after agreeing to go to lunch, I wrestled with second thoughts as I paced my bedroom trying to choose what to wear. One anxious hour and a pile of rejected outfits later, I headed out the door to meet him for our date, already certain we would just be friends.

Climbing into his immaculately clean truck, I envisioned with chagrin the kids' old waffles that I had found while cleaning out my car that morning. On the surface, we definitely weren't a match made in heaven.

Phil started driving and chatting while I wondered where we were going. After a few minutes, he told me we were stopping at the mall for lunch because he needed to buy some socks. As we sat on a bench outside the restaurant waiting for our table, I tried to figure out how I felt about shopping for socks with him. As conversationally as I could muster, I asked him if he was looking for a special kind of sock. He burst out laughing and told me he was kidding about the socks.

There he was. The real Phil had finally turned up. His grin and his sense of humor were infectious, and I spent the next several hours laughing, feeling light and happy. When he left my house after our date, I couldn't stop smiling.

By the time the 2000 track season started, Phil had asked me to marry him. I said yes, despite the fact that we had gone on our first date only one month earlier. My cautious, sensible self was overrun by the irrational yet undeniable certainty that I wanted to spend the rest of my life by his side.

For the entire track season, we kept our engagement secret — avoiding whatever well-meaning advice we might get from people concerned we were moving too fast. Eventually, we astonished everyone we knew with the announcement of our June 2000 wedding. We were married on a hiking trail surrounded by a small group of stunned family and friends. Since Phil hadn't been married before, I wanted to surprise him by wearing a wedding gown and a veil to our casual outdoor ceremony. The look on his face when he saw me that day still lives in my heart. He was glowing with love — and that eclipsed the gaping mouths and doubtful glances of some people around us. Each step I made down the dirt aisle that took me to his side increased the growing certainty I felt that life was about to be really good.

Chapter 4

The Trauma
That Changed Me

For the majority of our marriage, Phil and I lived with a varying number of our children on a quiet street tucked into a sleepy neighborhood. No one drove down our street to get anywhere but home. Our driveway was wide and sweeping and provided the perfect space with which to create a basketball court to keep our blended family of eight entertained. The house we bought came with a garage-mounted basketball hoop, and we added a second standing hoop to create a full court. One of my favorite things to do was to look through our large picture window while I made dinner and watch the kids play basketball together.

The kitchen in the home Phil and I shared was sunlit and warm with north-facing windows that overlooked our large, open driveway and brick-wrapped front yard. None of the kitchen windows were covered by blinds or drapes when we moved into the house. From my first glimpse out of those windows, I loved the uninterrupted view of the front yard. I enjoyed the openness of the space so much that during a home remodel we decided to allow the windows to remain bare in order to capture as much sunshine as possible and retain the front yard view.

A love of basketball was one of the very few things on which all six of our kids could agree. Blending a family is a tricky business. Phil and I came to our marriage with two boys and one girl each. His kids ranged in age between twelve and sixteen and mine between six and nine. I was divorced after a marriage of seven years, and he was three years past the ending of his longtime relationship with his kids' mother. In the early days of living under one roof, the basketball court was the only place where a peaceful blending of our family felt even a little bit possible. Many of my evenings were spent listening to the sounds of Phil rallying the troops for a game while peeking through the window to see one child or another flying through the air, intent on achieving the elusive slam dunk.

Often the soft sound of the opening and closing of a bed-room door, followed by the crashing slam of the front door, was a part of those evenings. This sequence of sounds signaled that whichever kid had been resisting participating in a fam-ily activity was now fully enticed, by the noisy banter that ac-companied every game, to join the competition. Phil was like a magnet. If all six children were home, the basketball court would eventually be overflowing with my husband, all six kids, and laughter.

Parenting is hard. Stepparenting is next-level hard. Phil and I both struggled to understand each other's kids and also to find a middle ground from which to co-parent. His kids were annoyed to have three little kids and a stepmom added to their family. My kids desperately wanted to be loved and accepted by their new siblings and new stepdad. Fights, misunderstand-ings, judgments, and going to bed angry were definitely part of our blending experience. Through many difficult parenting moments, my dreams of creating a harmonious family unit were framed by that large picture window. The view from my kitchen was full of camaraderie and possibility. I did not know that the peace and hope that flooded through our window grids would be short-lived.

My kitchen view was turned upside down one sunny August evening.

August 31, 2005, was the first day of school for my three kids. My eldest, Caitlin, was entering her first year of high school, and my youngest, Joshua, was beginning middle school, accompanied by his brother, John, who was the only one of the three returning to a familiar campus. Phil's oldest son had just begun working with him, and his siblings would begin school in two different locations a couple of weeks later. The fall season was a busy one for our family. That Wednesday was a lovely late-summer day spent planning for Phil's fortieth birthday, which was two months away. During my lunch break I booked the party venue, the adult bounce house, and the margarita vendor — who was not at all concerned about the pairing of a bounce house with free margaritas.

As I was jumping in the car to pick the kids up from their first day of school, Phil called to check in. After some idle chatter and a bit of venting on my part over a tough work situation, Phil told me that hearing my voice was the best part of his day. I laughed and told him that he was the only one I could imagine finding joy in my complaining. I hung up with a smile on my face and headed out for day one of carpool duty.

After we dropped off several other students at their homes, my kids and I enjoyed our traditional first-day-of-school ice cream stop and then headed home. I can still picture us walking up the driveway, everyone talking at once, as Phil stepped out of the garage with his mountain bike rolling along beside him. His helmet was on his head but not strapped, and he was clicking along the concrete in his cycling shoes. He waved to the kids, who threw their hellos over their shoulders as they ran inside to free themselves from all things school related.

Phil and I chatted briefly, then he kissed me goodbye quickly as he headed off to meet his friend Dean for their usual Wednesday evening ride. I can almost hear the click of his helmet strap buckle as he took off down the street. The vision of him riding past our neighbors' homes with a wave to this one and a hello to that one lives in my memory like a grainy video. I didn't know that would be the last time he would kiss me, the last time he would smile over his shoulder as he rode away with a joke and a laugh.

The pile of first-day-of-school forms that needed signatures was in the middle of the kitchen table, chicken was sautéing on the stovetop, and I was glancing over client notes for my evening personal training session. Caller ID was pretty new, and as the phone rang, I absentmindedly glanced at the number and realized an unknown cell number was calling. I almost didn't pick up the handset, but curiosity drove me to answer. A female caller asked if I was Michele, and after I confirmed, she told me that my husband had been hit by a car. She stayed on the line just long enough to provide her location and to encourage me to get there as fast as I could. As I started to ask if he was okay, she hung up.

My eyes were drawn to the kitchen window as I stood for a moment listening to the dial tone and trying to comprehend the words floating around in my head. *Hit by a car.* A vision of Phil's jaunty wave as he headed down the street less than an hour before came to mind, and I rushed into action. My mind reasoned that since a person from the scene of the accident called me instead of 911, Phil's injuries must not be life-threatening. In my shocked state, the idea that she would have called both me and emergency services didn't occur to me. I did not imagine — as I told the kids that Phil probably broke his leg, called a friend to sit with them, grabbed my keys, and ran out the door — that the view from my kitchen window would never again be the same.

The accident happened about three miles from our house. As I drove the city streets, I repeatedly took my foot off the gas pedal to keep myself from speeding up the hills that were populated by several cyclists. Each time I passed a person riding a bike, my desire to rush to my husband's side increased. The woman on the phone told me where to find him, but as I drove, I was shaking and scanning the road, looking for signs of him at every turn.

When I finally approached the scene of the accident, there were several parked cars and a handful of people standing by the roadside. I didn't see Phil anywhere. Desperation began to rise as I looked from face to face, asking each one with my eyes, *Where is my husband?* A familiar voice called my name, and I looked over to a patch of grass where Dean was leaning over Phil's unconscious body. I ran to his side. As I knelt over him, I was relieved to see that he was breathing. He was covered in cuts and his wrist looked broken, but at first glance every injury appeared to be repairable. Then I noticed that Dean was holding a blood-soaked handkerchief to Phil's head.

The vision of my beautiful husband lying on that grass is permanently burned into my memory. Though the patches of road rash and open wounds were severe, the pained look on his face concerned me the most. His breathing was shallow, and he was lying completely still. Kneeling beside him, I kissed his head and whispered words of love into his ear. When he heard my voice, he turned his head toward me, confirming that he knew I was there beside him, loving him and willing him to live. That moment, that small head turn, has remained an invaluable gift.

Our quiet exchange of love was quickly swept away by the wailing sirens of the emergency vehicles, the meticulous efficiency of the team of paramedics, and the strapping of my dark-skinned Greek god to a sterile spinal board. I sat in the grass with my knees pressed to my chest watching as the various teams worked. He never moved; they were breathing for him, and icy fear consumed me. I tried to console myself with the thought that Phil was strong; I often teasingly called him my Superman. Stubbornly, I squashed my growing feeling of dread as someone led me to the waiting ambulance and placed me in the front seat.

As we flew toward the hospital, the back of the ambulance was eerily silent. Sitting perfectly still, I could almost hear the lights and sirens screaming the word *emergency*. When the ambulance finally came to a stop, the small door separating me from Phil was thrust open, and I was firmly asked to stay in my seat. Stepping around to my side of the cab, the driver of the ambulance looked me in the eye and said, "I am not very good at this.... I am so sorry." The EMT kept talking, but all I understood was the fact that her lips were moving.

The inner turmoil caused by her words did not break my outer facade of calm, nor my stubborn certainty that Phil was going to be okay. As we stood in the driveway, I asked if I could go into the hospital room with my husband. After having to repeatedly insist that I could keep myself together while they worked to save him, I was reluctantly led by a kind nurse through the staff entrance of the hospital.

Entering the emergency room bay, I immediately sensed the tension in the air. The nurse led me into a room full of hospital staff performing what looked like a dance. Every person knew their part as they stepped in and out of one another's way with ease; I was momentarily mesmerized by the synchronization of what they were doing. At the center of the activity, Phil was lying on the gurney with his clothes cut off. I stood at the foot of the bed no longer able to deny that his life was in danger.

Phil's skin looked gray, his open eyes were vacant, and nothing anyone did was getting a response from him. The bottom of my world dropped without warning, and I felt like I was plummeting as my heart was being torn from my chest. I wanted to cry out, "Please, please save my husband!" But my sensible self was still somehow in charge, and I knew that if I caused a scene, I would be forced to leave Phil alone, and scared, in this room of dancing strangers.

Shakily, I stood at the end of the gurney with my fist in my mouth, biting down hard while tears ran down my face. The doctor shocked Phil's chest with electric paddles, and I watched his body lift off the bed with a mixture of hope and fear. Every shock Phil received reverberated through my body as if it were happening to me. Desperation gripped me as I listened to the medical team eliminate options for saving him. As I stood there watching in horror and disbelief, his life was ending. Frenzied minutes passed, and then the sense of urgency in the room began to fade into a sense of resignation — the change was palpable.

At that moment, one of my best friends quietly arrived. Ron stepped into my altered world just as everyone in the room ceased their activity and stood quietly as we watched the numbers on the heart rate monitor quickly drop — 54, 23, 14, 8, and then, finally, zero.

Doctors and nurses streamed out of the room, offering quiet condolences as they passed me. As I watched the emergency staff leave, I kept thinking they were making a terrible mistake — I wanted to run after them and pull them back to my husband's side. Turning to look at Phil, my final hope was shattered; lying on the gurney was only the shell of the vibrant man who had left our home one hour before. The silence in the room starkly contrasted with the screams of denial roaring in my brain and shattering my heart.

With surreal clarity, I saw the road my life would now travel. Like pictures in a slide show, my imagination displayed the variety of ways my life would be forever altered without Phil as my partner and friend. "No, no, no, I don't want to do this!" I screamed at Ron over and over. "I don't want to do this. He was just here!" I don't know how many times I moaned those words, but the horror of living without Phil crowded out all other thoughts.

As my screaming settled, Ron gently reminded me that we should make some calls. The poor man could see that he would need backup.

Ron stepped out to begin the process, and I was alone with Phil for the first time. I laid my head on his chest and wept. Though his skin was cold and its natural softness was gone, he looked very peaceful. I was amazed that his physical appearance was so swiftly and obviously altered by the absence of his energetic spirit. The only body parts I could see that looked unchanged to me were his ankles, so I moved down to the end of the bed and held them. At that moment, as my world was spinning out of control, I was anchored by the familiar feel of my hands on his skin. Outwardly, the emergency room looked exactly the same as it had when I entered thirty minutes before. Yet I knew that as soon as I moved away from my spot at the end of his bed, the landscape of my world would radically change. So, I just sat there, where the world was still a place I knew, holding on to my husband's ankles.

The business of death began immediately. There were time frames to be met and tasks to be completed. The next several hours passed in a blur of horror and disbelief. Phil's kids were at their mother's house that night. After I broke the horrible news by phone, two of them wanted the chance to see him. I sat numbly waiting for them to arrive, knowing that more heartbreak was on the way. I still had to tell my kids that Phil didn't just break some bones. No one should ever have to tell children that their father is dead. The screams of our children will haunt me until the day I die. All I could do was hold them, one by one, and try to convince us all that we would live through what felt like a waking nightmare. We were surrounded by the most loving family and friends, without whom I don't know how we would have survived, and yet we all knew that nothing would ever be the same.

Waking up to Phil's daily alarm the next morning, I was filled with dread at the thought of the number of days I had left to live without him. A warped version of the phrase "The first day of the rest of my life" popped into my head as I lay there consumed by the incomprehensible concept that Phil had been killed in an accident — an idea so surreal I could almost convince myself it was a dream. My body shook as I contemplated the suddenly empty world that awaited me. An imaginary specter stood in the doorway of my bedroom that morning, holding out a coat that was heavy and dark. As I passed out of the room to face the day, leaving behind the married woman I had been the day before, I donned the mantle of widowhood. There was nowhere to run; being a widow was not optional.

Chapter 5

You Can't Unknow
What You Know

On my first day as a widow, the story of Phil and me as a married couple ended and the story of me living through my husband's death began.

My marriage to Phil was one of the greatest gifts of my life, but if you had asked me before he died if my identity was dependent on my marital status, I would have laughed at the notion. Phil and I both had careers that we loved and were independently building our own businesses. We challenged and supported each other, but we also respected the fact that we were each doing separate and different work in the world. Our partnership was built not only on mutual admiration and respect but on a sustaining trust and belief in each other that allowed us to dream our own dreams.

After my divorce, I had worked hard to stand confidently in my own power. By the time Phil and I came together, any problems we encountered were met with two sets of solutions, mine and his. Sometimes I wouldn't tell him about a problem until I'd already handled the issue. My independent streak was strong and hard-won. Learning to compromise took time, and my stubborn independence caused several disagreements, but ultimately, Phil valued my strength and the fact that he could rely on me. Not that I had ever imagined life as a widow, but the last thing I would have expected to lose was my sense of self.

Guess what flew right out the window after Phil's death? Yep, my sense of self.

The day after my husband died, everything I knew about myself was suddenly and horribly in question. Slowly and consistently, my identity started to unravel, a situation that I found shocking and confusing when I wasn't crying or forgetting where I put the house keys.

The term *trauma brain* — also called *grief brain* or *widow brain* — is used to describe the total lack of mental acuity that often accompanies grieving the death of a loved one or processing any type of significant traumatic event. This safety net created by our brain shields us from the impact of severe distress, and it kicks in whenever we experience a traumatic situation. Slowing our mental processing and thereby limiting the amount of information we are able to absorb is the body's way of protecting us from mental overload. Our ability to remember, to calculate, to process complicated thoughts, to sleep, to read, and to communicate can all be negatively impacted by the emotional upheaval created by trauma.

After Phil's death I was terrified that my brain was gone forever. And I was right — just not in the way I imagined. My brain was protecting me from overload by creating a fog that rendered me barely able to function. If you are recently bereaved and are experiencing this low level of mental acuity and feel like you're swimming in a pea soup–like stupor, know that the thick fog does lift. This safety mechanism is normal. Yes, normal. This partial shutdown of the brain facilitates healing and provides respite. Rest assured, albeit slowly, functioning returns.

When it does, we are faced with a perception-altering truth: We can't unknow what we know. The reason trauma changes us fundamentally is because these experiences expose us to new understandings about ourselves and the world, usually related to things we would rather not know. This alters the way we think and often the way we live.

Prior to Phil's death, I knew nothing about planning a funeral. When someone at the hospital asked, "What funeral home would you like us to contact," I just stared blankly and wondered why they cared, and if there even was a funeral home in Simi Valley. Prior to Phil's death, my life did not include the words *blunt force trauma*, and though I had been trained in CPR many times, the only actual use of CPR I'd ever witnessed was on a television show. In the world I used to know, my loved ones were safe from harm, and the sound of an ambulance siren was background noise on my daily commute.

Standing beside my husband as his life ended made some universal truths crystal clear. People die, and the ones we love are not immune. Seems simple, right? Of course people die. The difference is that I suddenly understood that *my* people could die on any random Wednesday. The ones I love so much and feel I can't live without. Before Phil's death, I truly believed that there was no problem that couldn't be solved with cooperation and determination. In the universe of Michele, if you worked hard and stayed the course, anything could be achieved.

The day I realized that no amount of hard work would change the fact that my husband was dead remains one of my clearest memories of this time. Sitting at home in the office I had shared with Phil, having just sent the kids off to school, I was attempting to sort through his business paperwork. Seeing his handwriting on the calendar and business planning documents was making me cry, and I was giving myself a stern talking to about the need to get something useful done.

Drying my eyes and returning my gaze to the piles of messages to return and decisions to make, I thought about the hard work Phil and I had put into laying the foundation for his air-conditioning and heating business. He was scheduled to take the test for his contractor's license three weeks from the day he died. Phil was not a great test-taker, and he was super-nervous about the exam. He and I had spent many evenings on test preparation, with me quizzing him from flash cards and him either answering seriously or making up ridiculous answers that made me laugh out loud, while I scolded him to stop fooling around.

Holding the now useless flash cards in my hand, thinking about our many business conversations and study sessions, I realized that there would be no successful completion of this project. A business would not be built and our dream would not be achieved. No amount of effort or staying the course would return Phil to my life.

The reality that neither dedication nor determination would change my fate was horrifying to me. A tenacious mindset was my go-to method for improving my life, and this time nothing was going to alter the course set for me, one I did not choose and did not want. This was my first understanding of an irrevocable shift in myself. Not being able to hard-work myself out of this situation left me uncertain and afraid.

This unfamiliar daily fearfulness caused an increasing level of insecurity, which led to sleeplessness, a low level of anxiety that accompanied me everywhere I went, and sometimes full-on panic attacks. I hated being anxious. I hated the way fear made me feel. I hated being uncertain. I hated lying awake, every single night, wondering if I'd locked the door. I hated watching my kids walk out the door with icy fear gripping my insides, as I did my best not to cling to them while issuing a stream of warnings about how to stay safe during the day. I started to hate myself.

No matter how I tried, I couldn't unknow what I now knew. I couldn't believe or even pretend that my life might not be changed by another trauma tomorrow. There was nowhere to run and nowhere to hide. That's the life-altering part, knowing that if what happened to me was possible, then something else might occur that was worse or harder or even just the same amount of hard. I knew, no matter how much pain I felt, that there was a good chance I'd have to live through something awful again.

Take a moment now to consider what you have lived through. What happened? Name the trauma that has changed you. These life-changing experiences leave footprints on our heart, and they change our perspective. What do you know now that you didn't know the day before tragedy struck? In what ways has this new understanding changed the way you think, the way you feel, and the way you see the world?

In those early days, as I struggled with not being able to employ my regular strategies for problem-solving, what dawned on me was the reality that so much of what I used to believe, naively but firmly, was no longer true. My new self understood that people die, because I had watched my husband die. I knew that experience would never leave me. My trauma-influenced self realized that things don't always work out and that our worst fears may become our daily reality. This knowledge was now personal, and this knowing changed the way I lived in the world. Suddenly, the risks associated with living felt huge, and new fears jumped out from around every corner. My inability to cope with daily life, the physical manifestations of my new awareness (the anxiety, panic, and so on), and the changes in my can-do attitude headed the list of ways my post-trauma self felt inferior to the woman I was the day before Phil died.

I was not actually inferior, but I felt like a lesser version of myself as I struggled to cope with the varied symptoms caused by my lived trauma. Instead of recognizing the impact my experience had on every area of my life, I began to believe that I was irrevocably damaged. If you find yourself in this place, you need kindness and a break from self-judgment. Your previous standard of behavior needs to be set aside to make space for healing. Take this advice literally: Take a break right now, and give yourself as much time as you need before continuing.

Then, when you're ready, keep reading. In order to heal, we have to first feel.

Chapter 6

The Broken Vase Syndrome

Why should you learn to love a new trauma-informed version of yourself — the you who has been reshaped by some kind of loss? Why not aim for returning to the person you were before a tragic event or experience upended your world?

Because you have been changed by whatever experience led you to pick up this book.

We intuitively know this to be true whenever tragedy strikes, even when we resist that understanding. The journey of surviving trauma — through the many layers of body, mind, heart, and soul — asks each of us to take a walk of faith into uncharted lands. This chapter is devoted to a visualization that I suggest you do as you read. It focuses on the metaphor of a broken vase, which is a powerful expression of why a traumatic experience makes returning to a prior version of ourselves impossible.

Imagine a spectacular, colorfully patterned vase made of fragile blown glass. The vase is flat on two sides and about two feet tall. The lip of the vase has a clear, grace-ful dip that looks like a grin. Colorful patterns of red, orange, gold, green, and hints of blue swirl and wave within the soft glass. Visitors compliment the boldness of the colors and the incredible way that each hue stands out while also harmoniously forming the unique com-plexion of this piece of art.

This vase is a family heirloom that has been handed down through generations. It symbolizes your family history, and somehow it always lands with the person who is best able to understand the blending of history and beauty that is represented by this antique vessel.

The antique vase represents our life before tragedy. That life is both uniquely beautiful and complex. It contains everything that belongs to us, our history, our pain, our joy. The colors and shapes of the vase represent our life with all its imperfections and imbalances. These are familiar; we know them intimately, the ins and outs of our life. The vessel's swirls of color repre-sent the many parts of our personality, our personal history, the people we love, and the experiences that have shaped us up to this moment. Like the vase, imagine your life and your sense of self from before.

Next, visualize a family gathering on a rainy winter day. Grandparents and grandchildren, moms and dads, brothers, sisters, aunts, uncles, and cousins all attend. Food and laughter are shared by people of all ages. The meal is enjoyed, drinks are served, music is played, and revelry is in the air. An impromptu game of hide-and-seek commences, which includes chasing around corners, floor-skidding across tile, and warnings to take care while running indoors. Then a young girl wearing socks runs through the entryway, loses her footing, and slams into the pedestal that holds the vase. The girl cries out in pain, and all the adults hurry into the entryway just as the antique vase falls to the floor ... and shatters.

There is a moment of silence as everyone stares at the broken vase. Every family member, even the young runner, understands the significance of this vase. The child is unharmed, but pieces of the vase are scattered everywhere, all over the entryway floor. No one speaks, the child doesn't cry, as the enormity of what has happened sinks in.

The accidental breaking of the antique vase represents whatever traumatic event forever changes our lives. This can happen unexpectedly in an instant, in the amount of time it takes a vase to crash to the ground. Then again, at other times, tragedies can take a long time to unfold: The distance to the ground can seem endless as the fall happens in slow motion. However, once the vase crashes to the ground, there is no going back. Consider the moment your world shattered, as you regarded the pieces of your life scattered like broken glass on a tile floor.

The silence is broken by the child, who finally begins to cry. Adults reach out to comfort her while shouting warnings to the others to stand back from the shattered mess. Everyone agrees and understands that this was an accident, and they exchange expressions of gratitude that no one was harmed. It's just a vase. The girl looks up from the mess tearfully and asks if the vase can be glued back together.

Immediately after a traumatic event, there is a natural and often urgent desire to return to the life that existed before the tragedy. Everything is a mess, with pieces of what used to be scattered everywhere. When someone we love dies, this might include the loneliness of visiting a restaurant we used to frequent, the phone that no longer rings, the emptiness of our bed, or the sadness and concern written on the faces of others as they try to comfort us. The pull to go back to what was before is fueled by both the desire to avoid pain and the longing to restore what's been broken — the person and way of life we must now mourn.

I remember being awoken by Phil's daily alarm on the morning after his death. As the incessant beeping sounded, I kept my eyes closed hoping that he would reach over and turn off the alarm, thereby proving he wasn't really dead. All I wanted was the life that belonged to me just twenty-four hours before the chirping of that alarm clock. I felt just like the plaintive little girl in the visualization. All I wanted was someone to tell me how the vase could be glued back together so I could have back the life that was now broken.

The family gathers the larger pieces of the vase and sets them aside. Others use a broom and dustpan to collect the glass splinters and tiny shards, which are in every crevice of the tile floor. As everyone cleans up to make the entryway safe again, someone wonders aloud if the larger pieces might actually be put back together in some way. The original vase can't be re-created exactly, that's obvious, but maybe something can be restored.

Our lives — the vase — will never be the same after a tragedy, no matter how much physical or metaphorical glue is used. That reality is hard to swallow. Many people spend a lot of time and emotional energy working to re-create themselves in the exact image of their *before self*. Often, being able to return to one's before-the-tragedy self is viewed as a sign of healing — it's what so many of us yearn for.

As I experienced after Phil died, I couldn't help comparing my old, once-whole self with my new, still-broken self and finding my *new self* to be lacking. I longed to piece my life back together as if this tragic experience never happened, but that effort is doomed to failure. When tragedy happens and our life is shattered, pretending or acting otherwise is emotionally, physically, mentally, and spiritually damaging. We can't hold up a photo of the past and attempt to re-create that image or that self. Before and after can't be compared.

Bits of the vase, large and small, are placed in a pile and sorted. One of the older kids starts putting the pieces together in a new order, fitting them in unexpected ways. The glass, even broken, is still beautiful, and as the whole family sifts and joins in, they realize that they are no longer trying to save the vase. Together, they are making a new piece of art.

After a tragedy, we don't throw away what's broken. We undertake to form the pieces into a new life — one with its own beauty. This is where the work in this book begins. With picking up the pieces of your life. With gently sweeping up the mess left behind by the shattering. With building a new work of art from the remains of the old one.

In the following pages, you will be guided to gather the pieces of your life and gently hold and examine them. You will identify the value of each one and then stack and sort them into piles. You will carefully decide whether each shard fits or belongs within the new masterpiece you are creating. Some pieces will be large enough to form a foundation, some that hold particular value will be treasured, and some might not fit anymore and will be let go. You might discover that two unrelated pieces fit together unexpectedly well, while others might be too shattered to be used.

This is the work of rebuilding. By remaining open to new possibilities, we craft a new artwork out of our lives one small piece at a time. The only thing we know for sure is that, even though many of the pieces will be the same, this life won't look exactly the same as the one we lived before.

GRIEVE

Grieving Who
You Used to Be

Life-altering experiences cause fundamental shifts in our sense of self. The changes in our identity include the new traits and skills we learn that help us adapt to our new life. We might also discover unfamiliar emotional responses that are reactions to so much pain and suffering. Missing the person we used to be before a traumatic event is normal.

Chapter 7

I Miss Me

The person you were before the trauma that changed you is dead.

I know this is an extreme statement, but I believe that the key to learning to value and appreciate the new person we become after tragedy is to recognize and acknowledge the end of our previous way of life. Significant life events often become milestones or demarcation lines separating before and after. We each have our own. Whenever I am trying to remember when something happened, Phil's death is my primary time stamp. I think of events as before-Phil or after-Phil. This is one demarcation point on my personal timeline.

Wonderful events like the birth of a child or the purchase of a first home also become life markers. These are also before-and-after moments. The main difference is that, in general, these positive events reflect what we want to happen; they fulfill our desires or make our lives better than before. Trauma, meanwhile, represents unwanted change. Tragic milestones often, but not always, represent events that diminish, challenge, or change us in ways we don't expect or want. We don't literally die, but our dreams for the person we hoped to be have died, and we must recognize that loss in order to move forward.

The first step for beginning again is to accept that the life we led before has ended. Mourning the person we used to be, and the life that we used to live, is normal and necessary, especially when the changes in our life weren't asked for or anticipated. When something of value is taken from us, a full range of emotions follows — including anger, fear, and sadness. Grieving what was is healthy and helps us learn to fully embody the person we are becoming.

In the first months after Phil's death, the lethargy, absent-mindedness, deep sadness, apathy, and listlessness I felt made sense. I ached for Phil in every inch of my body, and I spent any energy that was left after a day of caring for the kids, working, and managing the household, missing him. The great void created by his physical absence was my go-to reason for why my life and my sense of self weren't the same. I felt relief at first to be able to point to a reason outside of myself for the mental shifts I was experiencing. I viewed these differences as temporary, as if I'd picked up a few tics that would be worked out once I got back to normal.

As time marched on and I got further and further from the day of Phil's death, I became discouraged and confused by my lack of drive, continued forgetfulness, and constant indecisiveness. These lasted to varying degrees for years. Those first years were mostly spent wishing the old me would come back. My conversations with myself at that time all included some kind of comparison to my self from before, and none of them were complimentary.

I missed the person who knew what she wanted, without

having to check back with me-myself-and-I ten times to be sure.

I missed the person who thought of herself as a Pollyanna type. You know, the one who always believes that all things will work out for the best.

I missed my brain. A lot. The lack of functioning, especially my sudden inability to multitask, was so annoying.

I missed the person who didn't assume that if a phone call wasn't answered, the person being called was surely dead.

I missed feeling sane and seen and valued.

I missed living with a strong, funny, hot, reliable husband by my side.

I missed knowing my husband was waiting for me whenever I returned home from a trip away or just a trip to the grocery store.

I missed feeling courageous and bold, the kind of woman who would marry a man she'd been dating for six months because she felt so certain that marrying him was her destiny.

In fact, I still miss that me. She was cool and funny. She was hopeful and believed that she was in charge of her own destiny. She took risks without a lot of second-guessing and found ways to work things out if they went awry. She lived with an ease and naivete that was beautiful.

Then her husband died, and so did she.

I was devastated by the loss of this self. I did not want the life I saw ahead of me. When I cried out, "No, no, no, I don't want to do this!" in the emergency room standing at the foot of the bed where my husband's lifeless body lay, I knew exactly what I did not want. I did not want to be changed. I did not want to become a new person. I did not want to build a new life. I definitely did not want to build a new life without Phil. I felt like someone stole my best self and left me with a lesser model that I didn't like or want.

The disdain I felt for Michele version 2.0 was constant. This girl couldn't do anything right. She couldn't cook a meal for her kids without forgetting some vital ingredients, like the chicken needed for baked chicken. Even when I did have all the necessary ingredients for making baked chicken, I sometimes forgot I was cooking at all and ended up with accidentally blackened chicken, which the kids liked to call hockey puck chicken. That's when I called for pizza. In fact, the new version of me was on a first-name basis with the pizza-delivery people.

My new self couldn't read more than two sentences without having to go back and reread for comprehension. She missed appointments of every kind despite having written them in her calendar, on a sticky note, and on the family whiteboard. New me was impatient and prone to tears, and anxiety was her constant companion. Try as I might to return to my prior way of thinking and to push past the fears that were now a part of my everyday life, I just couldn't. And I judged myself about failures large and small every day.

What I didn't realize was that I needed a new way to gauge my progress. I was measuring myself by the yardstick of another life, and I was setting myself up for failure again and again. The desire for my old life was so strong that I made returning to my old self my primary goal. I wanted to leave behind the coping techniques I was using for my pain and to train my brain to act as if the trauma had not changed me.

I didn't only want the old me back. I wanted her entire life back. My grief was not only for my husband but for the great life we had been living together. This was the life I had chosen, the life where I felt in charge even when things were hard, the life that represented the version of myself that I respected and valued.

Grieving ourselves can feel similar to mourning another person. We ache for specific traits and qualities we were proud of that might be missing now. We long for the naivete that accompanies the innocence of the time before. We may daydream about life as it used to be, and the people, places, and things that populated that world. Saying goodbye is hard, especially when the goodbye is precipitated by a pain unlike any we've ever known.

Once we accept that our life won't be the same and that the person we are after trauma knows and feels things our prior self did not, we open the door to getting to know our new self. We may always miss parts of our old life and our previous self. We may always feel a yearning when we think back to our pre-trauma lives. We will miss and yearn for the version of ourselves that has died the same way we miss and yearn for a person who has died.

Pause and reflect if you find yourself saying, "I wish things would get back to normal" or "I wish I could forget this horrible thing happened." Instead of judgment, offer yourself some grace. Allow yourself time and space to grieve — for the life you once lived and the person you once were. And put aside any judgments about the person you are now, the one still coping with pain and trauma. If you are having trouble with offering yourself kindness, the next chapter is meant to help. After a traumatic event, your life and your sense of self will be different, but that doesn't mean they will be inferior. In time, you might find your new life isn't just adequate or merely good, but even great.

Take a moment to reflect: What do you miss about your pre-tragedy self? How was that version of you totally awesome? Think about the way that person walked in the world. Consider the differences you see in the way the current version of you manages life. What parts of the life you used to live do you miss the most?

Chapter 8

When Is the Old Me Coming Back?

Tragic experiences create a dividing line between our before-tragedy and our after-tragedy lives. Often the difference is shocking, and the shock waves reverberate through every area of our lives. Even when a tragic event is expected, the resulting life changes — particularly all the challenges we didn't choose or volunteer for — can be both frightening and disorienting.

After a life-altering trauma, even as one version of ourselves dies, another version of ourselves is born. The birth of this self takes place at the moment of the trauma, and it's not a pretty birth. There are no birds singing or people celebrating the entry of this new person into the world. Instead of joy and expectancy, there is pain, confusion, and sorrow.

This is another reason we often unfairly compare our former self with our present, post-trauma self. Our new self doesn't stand a chance because the grass will always be greener in the past, before the trauma occurred.

The new person born by trauma typically arrives into what

is likely one of the most difficult chapters of someone's life. If we try to just suck it up and keep moving, it's almost like telling a newborn to figure out how to survive on their own, with no help, no guidance, no love, and no kindness. If we judge our new self harshly whenever we fail to cope, we are forgetting the crushing burden we are under and all the many advantages our prior self enjoyed.

Like chapter 6, this chapter is devoted to a guided visualization, one that's meant to embody this dynamic. As you read, imagine yourself as both persons in this scenario: as yourself and as the person to whom you give an impossible task. These are your pre-tragedy and post-tragedy selves. Pay attention to how you feel and to what parts of this scenario resonate most strongly with your own experience.

Several days after a traumatic event, you visit the person who was in the middle of the tragedy. They are emotionally wrecked and bone-tired. Their eyes are vacant, and they seem disoriented. Their feet seem weighted by cement blocks. They have been either unable to sleep or mired in exhaustion, sleeping all the time. Their memory is unreliable, and they wear their pain like a second skin. Each day, they experience a different face of the trauma, perhaps anger, depression, apathy, or something else altogether. You love this person, but looking at them hurts your eyes, and you feel it's time for them to start moving forward. They need to leave this place of pain and restore their previous life.

You both stand at the base of a steep hill; on the other side is the destination, the place where the person can become who they were before. The landscape is dry, with nothing green in sight. The path on which you stand

is paved, and the incline is so severe that you feel as if
you are leaning forward while standing upright.

In the immediate aftermath of a traumatic experience, the situation often requires instantaneous action and management, but we may feel incapable of making decisions and unable to cope with our circumstances. As our struggles continue, we can become increasingly disoriented, disheartened, and frustrated. We don't recognize ourselves or the landscape we are in, both of which have been transformed by tragedy. Our first impulse can be to force ourselves to get over it and get back to the person we were.

While standing at the base of the mountain, you start
filling a huge backpack with heavy rocks. Each is labeled
with a different word: fear, guilt, shame, regret, pain, disbelief, withdrawal, disappointment, disillusion, disapproval, *and so on. You keep stuffing the backpack with*
as many rocks as you can find until it is full, with no
room inside for anything else. You pick up the bag, which
takes all of your strength, and place it onto your loved
one's shoulders. The weight of the pack bows their body,
but somehow they hold it and don't fall over. The person
accepts that they are required to carry this burden.

In the days, weeks, months, and even years that follow a traumatic event, we experience strain, stress, and emotional upheaval. These feelings are related to the specific events we've gone through, and they also arise from our self-judgments whenever we don't measure up to how we think we should act. If we agree to carry these feelings, they become like rocks in an enormous backpack we must take wherever we go. Our new self is burdened from the first moment of their existence, and this self continues to add more rocks of all sorts along the way.

Now you tell the person to start walking. The only instruction you give is to follow the path until the trail ends. There is only one road, and it only travels one way, straight up the mountain, with several sharp turns and sheer climbs easily visible. The distance to the trail's end is not clear, but the difficulty that lies ahead is unmistakable.

In the short term, upheaval is rarely followed by a period of quiet. We may face a long, urgent list of tasks, perhaps involving hospitals, ambulances, social workers, police, lawyers, funeral homes, and others. These tasks are required. There is no way around them, and they might be both unfamiliar and daunting. Despite our many emotional burdens, we have to deal with them. In addition, regular life continues, with no break. We have jobs and people who depend on us. The call of daily life whispers or screams, depending on the urgency of the issue at hand. So we start walking, despite the steepness of the path and despite not knowing how long we must climb or how far the destination is.

Your beloved person has no food or water. There is no room for any of life's basic necessities in the backpack, yet the person seems totally uninterested in sustenance. You become a little worried at this point about their physical well-being, but the person waves away all offers of help and marches forward anyway. They insist they will be fine and focus on the climb ahead.

Before Phil died, he and I maintained a schedule of regular meals. As a personal trainer, I was careful to balance my diet so that I consumed enough calories and nutrients to fuel my body for each day's physical tasks. I'd reached a point where my body would respond like clockwork to the need for food. You didn't want to mess with me if I'd missed a meal! The day after Phil died, I couldn't be convinced to eat, and in the following days the refrain around my house, uttered in varying tones by my support network, was "Just take one bite, please." After about a month I realized that I'd hardly eaten, and yet my body wasn't waving any warning flags. I didn't get the usual headaches signaling a need for food, and I didn't pay any attention to the frequency of my meals. At the time I remember being stunned by the fact that my body didn't notice a lack of nutrition. I didn't yet realize that this was just one of the ways that my body was processing the trauma of Phil's death.

The concept that my emotional pain was drowning out my body's physical needs was foreign to me. I wasn't thirsty or hungry or tired in the same way that I had been just weeks before. Water and nutrition of any kind were afterthoughts; most often, people had to remind me to eat or drink. Though I was exhausted much of the time, my lack of energy didn't make me sleepy; instead I felt weary. The difference was stark and sometimes debilitating.

In the early days of a traumatic experience, pain and shock can mask our body's natural reaction to physical needs like hunger and thirst. Daily life is also often disrupted, so we don't have the reminders of our normal habits, like a regular noontime sandwich or morning coffee. In fact, if making coffee reminds us powerfully of the person we miss, we may avoid it, along with any other routines we shared. Trauma can imbue everyday acts with difficult emotions, so that dinner tastes like paper. The alteration of daily habits combined with the intense stress can make fueling our body an afterthought, if it's even a thought at all.

As time goes on, setting aside our physical needs can become a habit. Disordered eating, overeating, emotional eating, dehydration, and malnutrition are common by-products of living through a traumatic event. Absent the normal physical cues, facing significant emotional distress, and dealing with an overtaxed brain, our body's needs often fall totally off of our priority list. This lack of self-care then becomes a part of our daily life. Thus, we end up trying to overcome the most difficult emotional challenges we've ever faced without attending to our most basic physical needs.

As your beloved places one cement-booted foot in front of the other, swaying under the weight carried on their back, voices emerge from the edges of the trail. "Can't you move any faster?" "Ten years ago you would have been able to carry that weight with no problem." "You look awful." "Wow, you used to be so much stronger." "That was stupid." "What's wrong with you?" "How long are you going to use this pain as an excuse?" "Why do you keep forgetting things?" "You used to be better at everything." The jeers continue as the person struggles to keep going without collapsing under the backpack's weight or giving up. Then you realize there is no one else along the trail, only you, and the voice is yours.

This visualization represents how we often treat ourselves after living through a traumatic experience. Before we are ready, we give ourselves the impossible task of recovery, weigh ourselves down with negativity, and then judge ourselves harshly for not doing better. We measure our pre- and post-trauma selves and find the new version lacking without acknowledging the difficulties and challenges of our new situation.

Our pre-trauma self never had to face this climb — that is,

the unwanted challenges brought on by the traumatic experience. And that person never knew the pain we now know — the backpack of suffering, sorrows, and pain we now carry. After a tragedy, it is disorienting to wake up in terrible pain and to want to be the same person as before. Yearning to return to a familiar version of ourselves is understandable, but we only make our lives harder if we judge ourselves by our previous standards. We damage our self-worth by this unfair comparison of our pre- and post-trauma selves.

This is why letting go of the idea that we can return to an exact replica of our former self is vital. We are the person giving ourselves the task of meeting the steep challenges of our new life, and we are the one who walks that seemingly endless trail. The one who walks, who has experienced trauma, was birthed by that trauma and is in essence a stranger to our previous self, who knew only the greener pastures on the other side of the fence. We need to treat our new self with kindness, patience, and compassion, which lightens our burden. This new version of ourselves did not choose to be born and replace the old version, but through trauma, it happened. Getting to know this new person is a vital part of shaping the life we will build in the days, weeks, and years to come.

Take a moment and ask yourself: How are you treating this new version of yourself? Do you like yourself right now? Are you respectful and kind to the person who woke up this morning and had to handle the business of life no matter how heavy their burden? What challenges do you face today that would have been totally foreign to yesterday's you?

Chapter 9

The Dreams
That Left with You

Whether we are grieving the death of a loved one, the ending of a relationship, physical illness, or some other tragic event, this is always accompanied by a variety of secondary losses. Dreams, plans, and opportunities are all changed by the absence of that which we mourn. Identifying secondary losses and validating our feelings related to lost dreams is another step in the process of healing and rebuilding.

Immediately after a traumatic experience, it's common to be consumed by the trauma. The first days, weeks, and months are a time of shock as mind, body, and spirit begin the work of reconciling what has happened. The initial changes to which we must adapt are often the most dramatic, requiring alterations in our lifestyle, daily routine, and understanding of the world. The secondary losses are more subtle. They reveal themselves over time as we adapt to our new circumstances and put one foot in front of the other.

If we are grieving the death of a person, adjusting to the absence of their physical presence begins the moment we learn of their death, and it continues unrelentingly. We have come to expect and rely on the presence of this person in our everyday life, and we need time to comprehend the harsh reality that the person will never walk through our door again.

If the life-altering experience includes physical changes due to an illness or accident, or psychological damage due to a violent event, our first priorities typically include new and foreign experiences with doctors, experts, hospitals, law enforcement officials, and legal professionals. The list of physical tasks to be completed can take our focus and mask the secondary losses. This is another protective strategy employed by our brain, which allows comprehension to slowly build while the fight-or-flight response, activated by a life-threatening experience, retreats.

As the reality of our physical and mental state becomes clearer, a new daily routine begins, one that's altered by our experience. This reshaped reality highlights the ongoing influence of our trauma and its long-term impacts.

Until Phil died, my understanding of the impermanence of life was theoretical. His death made that understanding irrefutable. Yet, even facing the fact, day after day, that he wasn't coming home didn't prepare me for the many ways I would miss him for the rest of my life. My brain protected me from fully comprehending the enormity of his physical absence, which allowed me to adapt, bit by bit, to the changes ahead.

The first year of grief reset my life as I walked through anniversaries, birthdays, holidays, and life milestones without Phil standing beside me. When the second year began, I realized that this cycle of living through life events without him would repeat again and again. After the shock and disorientation of the first year, realization of my secondary losses began to surface. Our dreamed-of future together was no longer possible, and all the ways this was true became more evident with each passing day.

Secondary losses come in all shapes and sizes and can't be comprehended all at once. In the early stages of living through a trauma, the now is so important that tomorrow is pushed onto the list of things to deal with later. Yet eventually the time comes when we again think about and are forced to reassess our plans for the future.

Some people have very specific, detailed, big dreams, while for others the future is foggier. Either way, we all must make decisions about the culturally expected milestones that are peppered throughout our lives. These often provide a framework around which we shape our plans. These things include what kind of education to pursue; where in the world we might live; whether we will get married and have children; what career we will pursue; and where we might travel. The nature of a traumatic experience might affect some of these goals and not others, or perhaps our entire life needs to be reimagined and reshaped.

Dreaming about the future is a bit like writing a story. Every one of our life experiences shapes the way we imagine our future. Over time, as we visualize the life we desire, we make plans for achieving it. This includes anticipating the expected, normal challenges. For instance, if we want to be a doctor, that requires a long, expensive education, so how will we achieve that? What we can't anticipate are the unexpected tragedies and traumas that upend even the most careful plans. These are like dramatic plot twists that impact and change the rest of the story. Suddenly, after trauma, our imagined narrative has to be rewritten. That means letting go of the original plan for how our future was supposed to unfold.

Rewriting is hard. Almost by definition, our dreams

represent what we desire most. Letting beloved dreams go takes time and effort. In fact, it takes time to even realize all the ways that trauma will impact our plans. These are called secondary losses. Not because they are lesser, but because we only realize and appreciate them later, when the impact of trauma arrives in unexpected ways and forces us to realize how yet another part of our original narrative has been revised.

The day Phil died, I imagined, in a broad sense, all of the life he would miss. I knew the plans we had made together would never come to fruition. I saw all this as I sat in his hospital room: how much he would be missed at family events, during milestones in the kids' lives, and as a partner to me in both joy and heartbreak.

However, as devastating as this was, imagining him being absent was not the same as living without him when those imagined moments arrived.

Looking back, I think I did have a passing thought on the day Phil died about having a future grandchild whom he would never meet, but at the time I could not envision myself holding that baby in my arms. Eight years later, when that day arrived, and I stood breathing in the sweet baby smell of Phil's first grandchild, kissing the top of his soft head and introducing him to a funny-looking doll, my heart hammered and my eyes welled with tears. Phil was supposed to be holding his grandson. He was supposed to be there for that incredibly beautiful part of our story. For me, every part of that tender experience ached with his absence.

Each step of rebuilding my life after Phil's death highlighted a different dream that was altered or shattered by his death, and each new revelation required recognition, and eventual adaptation, as I wrote and rewrote a new version of the script for my life.

The expectations I had to release came in all sizes, from the assumption that our shared life would be managed by two people to the small realization that he would never see his beloved Raiders win the Super Bowl or experience the cool technology developed for the world of cycling. However, whether the losses were innocuous, like being unable to cheer for his favorite football team, or devastating, like never knowing his grandchildren, the list of dreams that would not be possible grew slowly but steadily. The more life I lived, the larger my awareness became of what I, he, and we were missing.

In your life, you are no doubt aware of how trauma has impacted your life's story in the most dramatic ways. Secondary losses are slower to reveal themselves and can't all be anticipated. These less-obvious alterations to your life plan will simply pop up over the years as you build and pursue your new life.

There is no way to know how many secondary losses you may endure. Like the original trauma, they often arrive unexpectedly, and you can't anticipate how you may feel when they do. Each loss can only be lived in the moment. Rather than count, catalog, or anticipate these future secondary losses, focus for now on your new life script. Focus on how you feel now, how you must adapt, and then begin the work of rewriting the story of your future.

Most people are familiar with revision. Whether writing a term paper, an article, an email, or anything else, we all struggle to find the correct word or the best way to express an idea. Every piece of writing has parameters and sometimes a word count, and it can be difficult and frustrating to fit what we want to say within them. That is an analogy for the task you face when rewriting your future. Right now, bring that struggle to mind, and sit with the feelings that come up. Imagine the annoyance and irritation of having to rewrite a paper that you liked just fine because a teacher said your essay was too long. The process of rewriting requires a sometimes-painful combination of patience, creativity, and determination.

Now, close your eyes and imagine that you've already rewritten the synopsis of where you are in your life at this moment. You've captured what you are feeling and how your life is different than it used to be. As you sit back from your keyboard and look at your screen, you see that it's displaying the right number of words, and you have also beautifully expressed what you intended to say. As you reread what you wrote, you see that paring down the words to their distilled essence forced you to choose only those that were most relevant to your process of healing and integration. The challenge of having to express yourself at this juncture provided the opportunity to consider your life from a variety of perspectives. Telling your story in a different way sparked new ideas and realizations — and your heart and mind will benefit from the effort. You've written a story that acknowledges what was, what is, and what can be. The work you have done has value and potential.

You will continue to rewrite your story as your life continues, since nothing ever turns out exactly as we expect. Be gentle with yourself if you get discouraged. Give yourself permission to take breaks if you feel overwhelmed. Though rewriting is often painful, the altered script may just be a masterpiece in the making.

INVENTORY

Discovering
What Matters

Before we begin to build a life for our new self, we must get to know the person born from the trauma. We must take a good hard look at the life we are living right now to determine the ways in which our current lifestyle supports or hinders our growth through the personal evolution ahead.

Chapter 10

Things That No Longer Fit

Getting to know our new self requires testing the norms that defined our previous life against the needs of the person we are becoming. Identifying and letting go of situations, hobbies, assumptions, and relationships that no longer fulfill our needs after a life-changing experience is a powerful step toward self-acceptance and building a new life.

How different or similar our new life will be from our "before" life depends, in part, on the experience we've lived through. If the trauma that has upended our world has taken away our job, our home, or our health, then these alterations in our life are clear and immediate. Someone's career may end because they are no longer able to perform their job's duties due to injury or illness, or someone's home and all their possessions may be destroyed by fire or natural disaster, leaving them without a house or any of the things that defined and represented their life before. Restoring certain physical possessions might be impossible, but more importantly, we must evaluate which elements of our previous life we want to keep or include in the new life we are now building.

When a loved one dies, many elements of our life may look identical or remain outwardly unchanged. Our home and job, even our immediate family, might appear unaffected. Yet inside, we may feel like our life is now totally out of order. The absence of this person from our lives might affect our passions and what gives us meaning. These changes may not be immediately obvious and can take time to make themselves known. As we build a new life for ourselves, we must consider how trauma has shifted not only future possibilities, but also many of our preferences, passions, and priorities.

A career that was once fulfilling could now feel empty. A hobby we spent hours immersed in may no longer hold our attention. Supporting a particular cause or volunteer work, which once played a key role in our sense of self, may no longer fill the same personal need. Trauma often causes a reset of our lives by forcing us to examine all the ways we spend our time, who we spend time with, and what we want to do with the time we have left.

Seeing things in a new way is a side effect of survival. Our experience provides us with a new, sharper, clearer filter through which we view our life and the world. We measure our current life and plans for the future against the trials of the past, and based on what we've learned as we integrate the impacts and lessons of trauma, we reshape that life.

However, despite this new filter or new way of seeing the world, what we do with this new understanding is optional. After trauma, a change in perception is unavoidable, but we get to choose whether or how to adjust our lives. Sometimes seeing things more clearly is uncomfortable. Where we live and how we live may suddenly feel wrong or confining, whereas it didn't before. We might question our priorities, our relationships, our interests, and our passions.

For instance, as a simple example, imagine that someone's favorite color was always blue, but now, for whatever reason, perhaps because of something related to their traumatic experience, they now can't stand that color. Yet their entire wardrobe is blue, and so a choice must be made.

Will they buy new clothes and slowly replace their wardrobe over time? Will they give most of their clothes away and only keep certain favored or sentimental items, despite their being blue? Or is blue now too upsetting, and so everything, their entire wardrobe, will go into the give-away pile?

The feeling of being out of place in a once-familiar world is very common after trauma. Looking around and suddenly wondering if our lifestyle is still right for us is natural after living through an event that has shattered our "normal" life.

We can sometimes feel that there is something wrong with us if our life before no longer seems to fit. The discomfort that nudges us to reexamine our life may be confusing or annoying, especially if all we want is to go back to the familiarity of what we've known. Feeling out of sorts in our current life may make us wonder if we're now broken in a way that can't be fixed.

If you feel this way, know that you are not irreparably broken. The emotional tug that is asking you to reexamine your life after trauma is a sign of healing.

You may not want to reexamine your life but you also can't unknow what you know. The nature of a life-altering experience is that it changes how we look at the world, and whether or not we do anything to integrate those understandings and change our life, the differences call out to be acknowledged.

That said, the call to respond and make changes in our perspective, priorities, or life circumstances can feel relentless.

And some people find themselves unable to change anything about their previous life, often because they want to hold on to the life they used to live as proof that they haven't been changed by trauma. When that stubborn holding-on happens, the only person who suffers is ourselves.

The brokenness we feel is a part of us and has lessons to teach. These lessons may be uncomfortable. Personally, I would have liked to have learned them in a different way. Yet if we allow ourselves to view the key areas of our life through our new lens, and we free ourselves from expectations, we will discover that this new world is full of possibility. When everything is up for grabs, what we reach for may surprise us.

Reevaluating our world doesn't necessarily mean changing every part of it. After a close examination of our day-to-day life, we might discover that our priorities still align with what we want to create in the future and that our previous lifestyle will still facilitate our continued personal growth. To know whether that's true, however, we must muster the courage to look at our lifestyle through the lens of our life-altering experience and ask this question: Is the way we've lived up to this point going to serve us best going forward, and if not, what needs to change?

Below, I review several areas that are commonly impacted by traumatic experiences to help you evaluate for yourself what might need changing for you and how. These areas include priorities, relationships, home and environment, and interests, including career, passions, and dreams.

Priorities

One of the most common and noticeable responses to traumatic experiences is the shifting of personal priorities. When struck with the sudden understanding that we don't have time to waste, we often focus on making more conscious choices about how we spend our time. If we discover that we have spent too much time working and not enough time hiking, we may find ourselves on a trail on Saturday morning instead of working on an unfinished professional project. If we've always felt called to run for public office, we may realize that the time is now. We can be filled with a new sense of urgency to accomplish the things we care about, and this can powerfully influence our daily decision-making as well as our long-term planning. Surviving trauma highlights the fragility of life and encourages us to make space for the people, experiences, and passions that fill and heal our hearts.

Relationships

The way we relate to people may also change, though these shifts can be complicated. In some cases, the impact of our new perspective may mean we become much closer to someone who was not a huge part of our life before. Meanwhile, if another person who used to be a regular confidante struggles to accept or acknowledge what we've gone through, we might feel less safe with them and confide in them less frequently. Our willingness to share our feelings openly can be impacted by our fear of the way others may respond. Especially when we are confused about those feelings ourselves. We may struggle to connect with family and friends afterward, or we may find that our experience and new perspective prompt family and friends to come together like never before.

People who knew us well may suddenly feel that they don't know us at all or that we are keeping something from them. Behavior that we once accepted as the norm may suddenly feel completely unacceptable. Our expectations of other people may change, and we may reassess the roles that family and friends play in our day-to-day life. While we are adjusting internally to the shifts caused by our experience, the people who love us must do the same. Some people may offer the patience and grace necessary to support a close relationship as we struggle to evolve into our new selves; others may not.

Often, people close to us can try to fix what they view as brokenness in order to help us get back to normal, to return to our old self, but that can be the opposite of what we need. Rather, we need friends and family to accept, embrace, and get to know the new person we are becoming, a person who has survived trauma. In all these ways, our changed perspective and priorities can influence the way we relate to people, the types of relationships we seek, and what we need and want from our existing relationships.

Home and Environment

When trauma occurs at home or in a space that is a large part of daily life, we may be unable or unwilling to remain in that space — the place where our life was changed. That physical space may no longer feel safe. To start fresh and begin a different life, we may want to do so from a new place. For some people, that might mean remaining in their current home but completely remodeling or changing the face of where they live. For others, it can mean moving to a new town or state and starting over in a location where no one knows their name or their story. Either option is viable so long as we settle our accounts with the place where the trauma occurred.

What does this mean? People often assume that physically leaving the place where hurt occurred is how they can escape or leave behind the experience itself. But the pain we've experienced lives inside us. We don't have to stay in the same space where the trauma happened, but leaving that place or transforming it is not going to make the pain go away, either. A change of scenery won't erase the reason for moving. Rather, in addition to whatever changes we make in our living situation, we still must do the work of emotionally healing from trauma, which might mean dealing with the painful associations a certain place has for us. Even as we move forward in a new location, the old one will always play a part in our life and in our future.

Interests: Career, Passions, and Dreams

One of the most significant impacts that a new perspective can have is on our dreams for the future and on our interests and passions. New things may matter to us. A lot. Surprising realizations related to our experience, people who have come into our life during our healing, and dreams that we were afraid to express before may all become of primary importance in the new world we are building.

Sometimes, other people can meet these new passions and dreams with resistance. They may regard a new hobby or cause, about which we knew little before, as a flight of fancy or an inexplicable obsession. They might be shocked by a decision to change careers after years of education and developing expertise in another field. What is absolutely necessary to us — the result of our changed perspective in the aftermath of trauma — may not seem obvious or necessary to the people around us. In fact, we may not be completely clear about how our priorities have changed; we just know they are changing. The new way we see the world — and the choices we make related to this shifting perspective — is an evolving experience influenced by our healing.

Every person is different, and every experience of trauma is different. How priorities, career choices, hobbies, passions, and dreams are influenced by these kinds of events will be unique for everyone.

What if your hope is only to restore the life you were living before trauma forced a rewrite to the script? Reevaluating our life in response to trauma doesn't necessarily mean changing every part of our life. For some people, their day-to-day lives might remain exactly as they were, and happily so. However, some things will definitely be different, and the differences call out to be acknowledged. Being able to recognize and describe those differences may take time. The key is to ask the questions and to remain open to new answers. This is how we build the life that fits our new selves best.

Give Yourself Time

The feeling of not fitting into your world can happen all at once or it may reveal itself over time as you do the work of processing your experience. The "old you" and the "new you" will share a lot of qualities. For some people, the two versions of themselves are so similar that outwardly no one would know the difference. Change for the sake of change alone is not the goal, nor is the aim to become a whole new person. Rather, give yourself the opportunity to make any alterations to your life that allow your new self a safe space in which to evolve and heal.

This time of questioning can be frightening. Where once there was certainty, uncertainty may now reign. What you knew about yourself without a doubt may suddenly be in doubt. If questioning comes naturally to you, this can be an exciting process. You may eagerly dive into new possibilities. If, instead, you thrive on predictability and certainty, this process may feel out of control and alarming. It can be easy to fear that wading through uncertainty will not lead to anything positive.

Whatever is true for you, offer yourself a huge amount of grace as you evaluate these pieces of your life. New lenses require a time of adjustment to avoid the headache caused by information overload.

When I was thirteen, I was prescribed my first set of corrective lenses. I remember the doctor telling me that my eyes would need time to adjust to my improved vision. He recommended I wear my new glasses each day for progressively longer periods: one hour the first day, three hours the next, a half day at the end of the week, and then finally all the time. Walking around with enhanced vision made colors pop, words on billboards decipherable, and everything I looked at sharper and clearer. I felt like I was seeing the world for the first time.

That same progressive approach can be applied to your life. The adaptations you will need to make to build a new life that you love won't, and can't, happen all at once. Take this process one step at a time. Listen to your body and your heart; they will both signal which area of your life needs attention at any given moment. This process doesn't have a deadline. Take the time you need to adjust to this new way of viewing your world.

Becoming the truest version of ourselves is a lifelong process of integration, in which the experiences of today become the lessons of yesterday, and the past influences how we live in the present and what we aim for in our future.

Trauma has a way of bringing common expressions to life — suddenly, smelling the roses can seem surprisingly important. The actions of people might speak way louder than words. And though you may not yet feel strong, or recognize your strengths, you have survived.

You are still here, and a life of meaning is calling you.

Chapter 11

Getting Back on the Bike

Phil and I shared a love of cycling. At least, you'd think so if you saw us riding together.

Before we officially met, Phil and I attended the same group bike ride while I was training for an adventure race in the summer of 1998. Newly divorced and having just been invited to join a racing team, I'd spent my savings on my first-ever mountain bike, and my teammates organized a group to join me and my new wheels on our maiden journey. Phil was part of the crowd of riders, and he told me later that watching me climb up the hills that day was the beginning of his growing interest in me. Not that anyone (including me) would have ever guessed, since he didn't utter one word to me beyond "hello" throughout the whole morning. Over a year passed before we eventually ran into each other in the hallway at the gym on New Year's Eve.

In the years after my divorce, I was testing out varying interests as I reshaped my life. Adventure racing was a new sport. I loved the friends who invited me to be part of their team, and learning to mountain bike was a necessary step for participating in the event that my team registered for. Riding for me was a means to an end that began with learning to navigate mountain trails on two wheels. Every single time I threw my leg over the frame of my bike, I took a deep breath and reminded myself that conquering my fears was an exercise in character building.

What Phil didn't know as he admired my hill-climbing skills was that riding a bike required me to push way past my comfort zone. I don't have a natural love of flying along, clipped in by riding cleats to a metal frame. I don't relish the rise in blood pressure that happens when leaning into a curve while riding down a mountain. I often struggled with a common concept for mountain bike riders: that you shouldn't look where you don't want to go. More than once, I peeked over the side of a mountain I was riding and ended up flying over the edge of said mountain, skidding along with my bike stuck to my clipped cycling cleats. But my mountain biking apprehension paled in comparison to the intense anxiety I felt when I imagined riding a lightweight, skinny-tire road bike, two feet (if you're lucky) from a car whizzing by at fifty miles an hour in the lane next to you. Yeah, not a fan.

By the time Phil and I started dating, training for endurance events was part of my everyday life, and while I still did not have a natural love of the cycling portions of the races, I probably looked pretty natural on a bike. Which is why he was sure that I should add road biking to my repertoire of hobbies.

Throughout our marriage, Phil and I regularly ran, rode, and raced together. Every weekend included some type of outdoor exercise, which we used as a way to stay connected to each other while parenting six kids. We were fortunate to have built a community of friends with whom we trained and shared countless athletic adventures. The group of people who would show up on any given day was influenced by scheduling and by who was injured that week, but we loved our large, dedicated group of friends who shared our passion for physical activity.

Our training buddies all had varied interests, and we often cajoled one another into committing to a new form of exercise. Before we met, Phil was tempted into road biking by a guy he admired who told him that road biking was a great way to increase cardiovascular fitness. Once Phil and I started mountain biking together, he began a campaign to get me to join him for road bike rides. He missed me when exercising alone, he said. He wanted to spend the hours he put into riding with me. He said he would teach me everything I needed to know, he bought me a road bike, and I reluctantly started riding on paved streets.

As the years passed, Phil and I spent some of our most memorable moments riding, running, or hiking side by side. I loved the way he believed in me. That is, except for the time when we were riding our mountain bikes at the Mammoth ski resort during the summer off-season, and without warning, he took me down what would have been a double-diamond ski run, which required me to jump my bike over a ditch and ride over a rope bridge. When we got to the bottom, I was as mad as a hornet, but Phil smiled smugly and said, "I knew you could do it."

In spring 2005, Phil became convinced that I could be a force in women's mountain bike racing, and he created a training program that would assure my field domination for the upcoming season. I was a reluctant participant in this plan, and to this day I feel fairly confident that an award-winning season would not have been a part of my future. But he could not be convinced otherwise. I still laugh when I think of the gleam that came into his eyes as he dreamed of my podium finishes.

Phil's plans for my racing career were never tested because just months later he died in a cycling accident, which realized one of my most intense fears as a cyclist.

His death reverberated through our local community and rocked the worlds of our cycling friends. Everyone knew that our sport could be dangerous, and most of us knew someone who had experienced a scary near miss or even a direct hit by a car while out for a ride. But until Phil died, few of us knew anyone who had lost their life while cycling. I will never forget exiting the emergency room on the day of his death to find a huge group of friends standing around the hospital doorway waiting for me. Every stunned face reflected the shock that someone they knew and loved was killed on a bike.

After Phil's death, the first few weeks and months passed in a blur. Nothing was normal, so I didn't notice the fact that I'd stopped riding my bike. In those days I was more focused on whether I'd fed the kids than on my daily physical activities. Exercise became an afterthought, along with my personal needs, as the weight of managing a life once shared with my spouse settled onto my shoulders.

However, as my new daily life took shape, one defined by the painful physical absence of my husband, I began to ache for the release that exercise provided. All at once I realized that I needed to be moving, and I began testing out each of our shared hobbies to see which one was the best fit for me without Phil.

Those tests were so painful. I have a crystal-clear memory of the first time I tied up my running shoes on our front porch alone. Tears streamed down my cheeks as a memory reel played in my head and Phil's voice reverberated in my heart. Taking a deep breath, I jogged down our street, passing the familiar homes of our neighbors and friends. I made it about fifty yards before I turned and walked home because I realized that I could not simultaneously run, cry, breathe, and see where I was going.

Eventually, though, I found solace in running. There was something reassuring about being able to pound my feelings through the pavement and the momentary relief of imagining outrunning the awful pain in my heart. I missed Phil with every step I took, and I also felt his presence with every mile covered. Running worked for the new me who was trying to find herself within the rubble of life after Phil.

Then there was cycling.

As I returned to running and hiking, many of our cycling friends who cross-trained joined me as a way to stay in touch after Phil's death. Anytime someone would call to check on me, I'd suggest a walk, hike, or run to catch up. Talking was easier if I could be moving. After a few months of this, my friends started to gently ask how I felt about cycling. Every genuine and sweet inquiry related to cycling was followed by an offer to ride with me, should I decide that I wanted to get back on a bike.

The phrase "getting back on the horse" haunted me during this time. I felt pressured to prove that Phil's death wasn't going to change the way I lived my life. I'd subscribed to the notion that the only way to prove that I wasn't "damaged for good" was to ride my bike again. I wanted my friends and family to know that I was brave and strong. I wanted to reassure them that I would make my way through this grief and return to my old self, the one they recognized. I'd decided that displaying that courage could only be done if I went on a bike ride. And not a mountain bike ride. I made myself get back on my road bike.

I can still feel the wind on my face and the terror in my heart as I stood in front of my bike that day. Trusted friends joined me; in fact, they picked me up at my house and took me to the place where we'd ride. I think that they might have been as afraid as I was of me being on a bike. We set out for an easy ride along roads with little traffic. As I threw my leg over the frame of my bike, the familiar feeling of anxiety swept over me. That part wasn't new. I always felt anxious when riding, but this time I was having a harder time valuing the concept of facing my fears as a character-building exercise. This time I wondered, as I headed out of the parking lot and crossed a street side by side with a car, why I was making myself do this.

As I rode along the street in the bike lane, I felt the disturbance, both physical and emotional, created by cars as they drove by. Each wave of air that hit my face felt like a punch to my chest. Each time a car passed I fought the urge to close my eyes. I kept imagining how Phil must have felt as a car collided with his beautiful Greek god–like body. How much of the impact did he feel? Did he know that his injuries would end his life? And why in the world was I riding a bike, terrified and miserable? To prove that I wasn't broken?

While on that ride I realized that I didn't have to prove anything to anyone but myself. The irony of using this ride to show that I was still the familiar me that others knew was that I never liked cycling in the first place. I began cycling simply to try something new after my divorce, and this accidentally became a hobby because my new husband loved it. I loved him, he loved riding, and so I rode. After his death, the only incentive I had for riding was not wanting other people to think I was weak and broken.

I thought there was something wrong with being broken. This was where my thinking went awry.

The truth is that being broken after a traumatic experience is normal and necessary. The traumas that change us also break us. The experiences that upend our lives can't be met with a business-as-usual attitude because business is anything but usual. Allowing ourselves to be broken makes space for the next logical step, the need for time to heal.

If we resist the urge to put our life back together "just the way it was" and instead ask ourselves which parts of our previous life still serve the person we are becoming now, our brokenness becomes our strength. We don't have to prove to the world (or ourselves) that we aren't broken. Embracing the reality that we've been changed by our experience provides a rare opportunity to recalibrate, to reflect, and to build a life that fits our new, post-tragedy self.

In the years after Phil's death, people became more comfortable asking me if I still rode my bike, and I slowly became more comfortable saying no. For a long time, answering this question caused me to squirm awkwardly and stumble over my words. Anytime this question hung in the air, my old self-judgment and second-guessing of my choice immediately returned.

Developing the ability to answer the question without embarrassment or guilt took a long time. Athletes are taught not to give up, and the athlete in me badly wanted to wear the badge of courage that I felt cycling after Phil's death would have earned me.

By leaning into both my brokenness and my healing, I discovered that, by making the choice to honor my own feelings and allowing other people to think what they may, I developed a different kind of courage. This type of bravery actually did build my character. No matter what anyone thinks of my choices, they are mine. I don't miss riding. I only miss riding with Phil.

Chapter 12

Filtering Feedback

After trauma enters our life, well-meant advice often follows. We can feel uncertain and unsure of what to do, the appropriate way to act, and the "right" way to heal, and it's natural to seek certainty. In this situation, the opinions of others, presented with confidence, even from people we don't know well, even from those we don't know at all and who have no experience in what we're going through, can suddenly seem very important.

The changes instigated by a traumatic experience impact not only us but the people around us. Our personal traumas are witnessed by family, friends, neighbors, colleagues, acquaintances, and strangers. Some of these folks may support us unconditionally, while others may be unavailable or even actively judgmental as we do the work of rebuilding.

One thing everyone has in common is an opinion about how we should manage our life and our healing.

Many people have an intense curiosity about the aftermath of trauma and how survivors make their way forward after their lives have been irrevocably changed. People watch carefully during this time of healing. When some of these people offer feedback, it's often fueled by genuine concern for the person's well-being, paired with a sense of helplessness as they bear witness to pain, especially if the person is someone they love. Others, meanwhile, share their unsolicited opinions, questions, criticisms, and judgments because they believe they know best — regardless of how the person feels or whether they want the advice.

After a tragedy, the intense interest and concern of others often leads to an overwhelming amount of feedback, and how we process this feedback can be complicated. Our self-esteem is often low, our situation is overwhelming and unfamiliar, and opinions and suggestions can arrive from every side. Filtering what is helpful from what is unhelpful, and then making our own decisions with confidence, can feel like a Herculean task. This difficulty often comes as a surprise, however. Compared to the trauma we've endured, we might imagine that handling the suggestions and advice of others would be easy, relatively speaking. When it turns into a quagmire, we can find ourselves feeling burdened in a whole new way.

Phil's sudden death drew an unexpected amount of attention from our local community. Initially, this was expressed by an intrusive parade of cars crawling slowly along our quiet suburban street. At first, I naively wondered what was happening nearby that was causing so many vehicles to be cruising our neighborhood, until the day an unfamiliar convertible idled in front of our house and the driver peered unabashedly into my kitchen window. My mind was blown by the idea that anyone would want to view the devastation that was my life.

While I still choose to believe that most of those folks

peering in my windows were well-intentioned, their actions made me feel vulnerable in a new and painful way. The basketball court that had recently held hope and promise became a gandering spot for lookie-loos, for all those people who felt the sudden need to keep an eye on me.

Suddenly I felt exposed in my own kitchen. Instead of contentedly viewing whatever was happening in my front yard, my days became a dubious game of peeking around the corner into the kitchen to see if anyone was driving by or standing on my doorstep.

As my feelings of vulnerability increased, I became hyperfocused on the practical ways that I could control my environment. After one too many cars slowly trolled my street, I ordered blinds for every uncovered window in my house. This one knee-jerk decision sparked an ongoing cascade of self-doubt and self-judgment. I knew I couldn't continue living like a goldfish in a tiny bowl, and doing something about it made me feel powerful, but I also felt as if I was giving in to fear and grief by literally shutting out the sun. The idea that I was surrendering to my need for privacy caused me to question the choices I made to protect myself and my kids.

I was so busy wondering if other people thought I was weak that I didn't give myself any credit for solving a problem with confidence. Covering the windows for the first time in five years created a sense of safety for my family, but the loss of that sunny kitchen view also represented another tiny way life changed the day Phil died. Today, I'm proud that I gave myself what I needed in that moment, and I wish I could go back and high-five that me.

The unwanted attention surrounding my home and my family lasted much longer than I expected. In the early days of cars rolling past my window, I felt sure that people would quickly tire of watching me grieve and go back to their own lives. Instead, I discovered that my life as a widowed, single woman drew unwanted attention long past the time I imagined anyone would care.

In public, as I went shopping and took care of chores, strangers felt comfortable inquiring about every personal topic imaginable. I received unwanted questions about parenting, grieving, dating, not dating, working too much, working too little, home repairs, major purchases, minor purchases, daily finances, the need to "move on," and more.

I walked away from countless conversations, dumbfounded by the brashness of the questions:

"How much life insurance did Phil have on himself?"

"Did you buy a red car to pick up men?"

"Do you really think you are modeling positive coping for your kids?"

At other times, I stood stupefied by the cruelty of statements made with matter-of-fact certainty.

"No one wants to be around someone who is so sad."

"Phil died six months ago — time to start fresh."

"If Phil really loved you, he would have taken care of you by having a life insurance policy."

At every turn, someone seemed to be watching what I was doing and felt free to drop their opinion in my lap, usually about topics that were none of their business — and I let them. Managing the onslaught of attention was exhausting; I was too tired to stand up for myself. Instead of setting boundaries, I hid in my house.

Trauma can take a significant toll on self-confidence. The reason that I allowed people to ask any question with impunity was my fear that they were right. My pre-trauma self made decisions with quick certainty and moved confidently from decision to action. After Phil's death, I changed my mind from moment to moment and second-guessed decisions immediately after making them. I lived under a chronic cloud of doubt that was distressing and maddening.

Even people whose opinions didn't matter to me at all drove my uncertainty to ridiculous levels. Why didn't Phil love me enough to buy a life insurance policy? Maybe I really was doing a terrible job of modeling healthy coping for my kids! Wait, did I subconsciously buy a red car to nab a man?!

Every observation, no matter who made it, caused my self-confidence to plunge. I finally shook myself out of that negative feedback loop — in which my damaged self-esteem was unable to filter everyone else's opinions and know my own mind — after experiencing a flagrant disregard for my privacy that took my breath away.

Six months before Phil's death, we decided that I needed a new car, and I fell in love with the recently released Mini Coopers. My previous cars were all practical, family-focused models designed to fit six kids. A Mini Cooper was definitely not that type of car, and I was reluctant to commit to a vehicle with so little space. Phil, however, loved the idea and kept pointing out all the ways that a Mini Cooper was the perfect car for me. He began a crazy campaign to convince me to buy a Mini that included pulling off the freeway whenever we passed a Mini dealer and insisting I go for a test-drive. He even rented a Mini Cooper for me to drive during a summer vacation that we'd planned and, because of his accident, never took.

After Phil's death, when I followed through on buying a new car, I had no doubt what kind he would have wanted me to purchase. In a rare show of confidence, I sold his work truck, put the cash in a new account, and ordered the car for which Phil had lobbied nearly every day for six months. A friend and confidante provided guidance and support while I ordered a red Mini Cooper with a black top and black interior. Red was Phil's favorite color. Choosing a red car made me feel as if we were both part of buying the long-awaited coupe. After handing over a cashier's check for the purchase, I felt settled. In that moment, I glimpsed my former decision-making skills — I was proud of myself for the first time in recent memory.

Then my phone rang.

An employee at the bank where I'd deposited the proceeds from the sale of Phil's truck noticed a large withdrawal from my account. He knew both Phil and me, and he called to ask me if I'd purchased a new car. Was the car fancy? Was the car red? Would I be speeding along in my hot little number?

My knees felt weak as I stood in my kitchen. I was stunned by the fact that this person knew I bought a car just one day after the purchase, and before the car had even arrived. How did anyone know what money came in and out of my account? Did I do something wrong? Should I have paid for the car a different way? Were my accounts compromised? A thousand questions churned in my brain like an agitating washing machine.

The person continued to ask questions about my purchase, and I answered them one by one, feeling like a teenager who was being quizzed after having done something foolish. Standing transfixed to one spot with the phone to my ear, I felt my newly born pride and confidence floating away. I had been absolutely certain about this purchase, and it now seemed not just questionable but irresponsible. Every doubt with which I'd wrestled during my sleepless nights roared back into my brain. I felt sick, sad, and ashamed.

Then, eventually, I got mad.

How dare this person access my personal financial information? Worst of all, this person had the audacity to imply that

Phil might not be happy with my purchase. I knew exactly how Phil felt about me buying that car. All at once, I realized that my reasons for any purchase I might make were no one's business but mine. I was in charge of my own life, for better or for worse, and in that moment I decided that I would no longer tolerate anyone else's inappropriate questioning. The realization that I was the only one tasked with making decisions for myself and my family arrived like a thunderclap. Anger gave me the courage to stand up for myself and to step off of the carpet onto which I'd been called.

Up to that point, I had allowed anyone access to my inner turmoil. As I wrestled with daily uncertainty, I sought input from anyone who wanted to provide an opinion, and I entertained advice of every sort. The more the better, I felt. Until more became too much, and I was mired in so many suggestions, judgments, and expectations that I had no clue what I wanted.

My overwhelming indignation provided me with the strength I needed to rebuild my personal boundaries. Just like when I bought the blinds, I shut out others in my world and made decisions solely on my gut. I did not allow unsolicited opinions to have any part in my decision-making process. My anger shook me out of the constantly nagging doubts that had plagued me, but shutting out people indiscriminately came at a cost.

After a while, I realized I was missing out on valuable input that might have saved me time, money, and heartache. I was now making every single decision for myself and for my family, but without any support or advice. Loving people wanted to help, but they were respecting my clearly stated boundaries. I needed to find a better way to filter the feedback I solicited and received, in part based on who each person was and what role they played in my life.

In the aftermath of trauma, people who can provide support, wisdom, and a listening ear are more vital than ever. After having overcompensated with my boundaries and struggling alone through one too many difficult decisions, I realized I wanted to be part of a team again. My original team, Phil and Michele, no longer existed, but others were willing to step up and help me create a new team. I needed to find a balance between total autonomy and unrestricted access — and I did.

In the next chapter, I explain the process I developed for identifying valuable advice, making decisions, and creating a supportive team.

Chapter 13

Life in the Fishbowl

Think of yourself as a goldfish in a clear bowl. You are in charge of creating and managing the environment that exists all around you. Can you see yourself there?

Using the analogy of the fishbowl, I have created a filtering method for prioritizing and processing recommendations and criticisms while building groups of support. For several years, I've been teaching this approach to help others as they heal from trauma, and I love the self-confidence it generates. It's all about creating an atmosphere that recognizes our independence without losing sight of the interdependence that is a vital part of the human experience.

To start, you need a notebook or a few clean sheets of paper. First, make a list of all the people who provide you with personal feedback, both positive and negative, on a regular basis. This includes family, friends, coworkers, neighbors — anyone who expresses opinions about the way you run your life. Most importantly, write down the names of those whose words have hurt you or whose opinions have made you question yourself, and also list trusted confidantes whose comments have challenged you to think of a topic from a different angle.

Then, assign each person to one of five categories or types of groups I describe below: fish feeders, fish who live in your bowl, fish in neighboring bowls, fishbowl viewers, and fish who live in the ocean.

Fish Feeders

Goldfish require feeding in order to survive. Since they aren't able to rustle up their own dinner, they count on their caregivers to be sure they are fed. Look at your list of people: Which of them feed you, whether emotionally, mentally, spiritually, and/or physically? Who would you turn to if you needed assistance with childcare or an extra set of hands for completing a task? Who would you call if you were stranded with car trouble? If you were sick and in desperate need of soup, who on your list would deliver that soup? In the case of an emotional breakdown, who would you call?

The fish feeders are your people. They are the ones who help you create and manage the environment in which you live. Fish feeders know you better than anyone else, and they are your core team, the people you can consistently count on.

The opinions of the people in this group matter. While their role isn't to make up your mind for you, their opinions, thoughts, and advice (even the unsolicited kind) are worth considering. This means that if they tell you something you don't want to hear, you should at least consider what they've said.

Fish Who Live in Your Bowl

What is your current living situation? Do you share your home with others? If you live with children for whom you are responsible, their opinions matter, too. People who live in your fishbowl are often impacted by the decisions you make. Hopefully, some of the people you live with are also fish feeders. Feel free to add people to both categories if that is applicable.

Feedback offered by the people who share your environment or home is a priority because the choices you make may have a noticeable impact on them. If someone you live with shares an opinion about a choice you are considering, think about whether and how that decision will impact them. Their suggestions or criticisms may not change the outcome of every decision you make, but it is important to take into account the effect your decisions may have on those who share your living situation.

Fish in Neighboring Bowls

List the communities you are part of. This may include social groups, religious groups, social media groups, support groups, and friends and family groups with whom you have a lot in common. These people are living life side by side with you. They aren't on your fish feeder list, so they are not part of your inner circle. These may be acquaintances or colleagues or groups of people you only see during the holidays. As for social media connections, these are people who mainly view your life through your newsfeed.

Neighboring fish often appear to be doing really well. When you glance into their bowl, all seems good, like they are rocking the goldfish life. They may have more coral trees than you do inside your bowl, or you may notice their water seems clearer than yours. In other words, we tend to compare ourselves, often negatively, to neighboring fish. They can appear to have exactly the environment we've strived to create in our bowl for years!

After a traumatic experience, it can become a torturous game to compare ourselves to people who aren't living through the same thing. Even measuring ourselves against others who have lived through a similar experience isn't useful. No matter how well others seem to be doing, our individual path is still ours alone. The lessons we learn as we create and re-create our individual landscapes are personal. Someone else can't learn our lessons and we can't learn someone else's. While we can definitely share our experiences and lessons, acquiring this wisdom is personal. Pay attention to how you process the feedback you receive from your neighbors — the ones who may be living a parallel life but are definitely not living your life. When you peek into other fishbowls, are they an inspiration or a hindrance?

Take the suggestions from "neighboring fish" into account based on how well you know the person offering the words of wisdom — for example, do you know someone only through social media, only occasionally or briefly, or only in a non-personal context? Then evaluate whether or not the advice they give you is practical and applicable for you. Even good advice that works for someone else may not be the right fit for you. Make your neighbors a part of your support network instead of making them your measuring stick. Keeping up with the Joneses is a losing game, even for goldfish.

Fishbowl Viewers

Following any tragic event, the watchers appear — just like the ones who drove by my house after Phil died. These are people who are drawn to the pain of others or are simply curious about how someone will manage the challenge they've been handed. They feed off of the need to know what you will do next! They are not a part of any of your support networks, and their feedback is often superficial because their opinions aren't based on any personal knowledge of you. Rather, they make general observations based on what they've seen while peering into your fishbowl.

Might they see something from the outside that you don't notice from the inside? Sure, but keep in mind that their perspective is limited. They only know what they have seen by watching from a distance. Also take into account that their impulse to watch others suggests a lack of attention to their own lives. This can be telling. The opinions of fishbowl viewers should be considered lightly, since the person providing this feedback doesn't really know you.

Fish Who Live in the Ocean

Salt water is life-threatening for goldfish. Any fish who lives in the sea cannot possibly relate to life in your fishbowl. This category is for people whose opinions are shared without regard to your feelings or the type of relationship you have with them — like that person you used to work with who liked to offer unsolicited professional advice or the coworker you've met twice who lets you know at a company party that you are putting out a "bad vibe." Add to this category anyone who doesn't know you, who hasn't lived through an experience similar to yours, and who has an opinion anyway. These fish live in the ocean; they don't get you.

Why create a group for these people at all? Because they can get under your skin. Because their words can cause you to question your decisions even after you've spent hours, days, or weeks carefully evaluating the best choice for you. Because when you allow ocean-dwelling fish to weigh in on your freshwater world, you are inviting feedback that (1) doesn't apply to you and (2) may be damaging to your ability to heal. If, comparatively speaking, people live in the ocean — leave them and their opinions way out there. You don't need them.

Create Your Fishbowls

Review the list you made of the people who populate your everyday life, and assign each one to an appropriate category. Write the designation next to each name on your list.

Then, when you are in need of advice or support, turn to your fish feeders, fish who live in your bowl, and maybe your neighboring fish. If someone criticizes a decision you've made or has a strong opinion about how to solve a problem, remember which category they are in. If they are fishbowl viewers or ocean dwellers, their opinions may not matter at all. However, if they live in your bowl or provide your dinner, carefully consider their advice before you act.

The purpose of this simple exercise is to provide a quick, lighthearted way to sort and consider feedback provided by all the people in your life. As a step-by-step process, it will help you avoid being overrun by the opinions, suggestions, judgments, and criticisms of other people. It will help you to quickly gain perspective and not give your power away to other people. Equally valuable, this way of thinking will help you avoid dismissing thoughtful feedback from the people who know and love you.

EXPLORE

Embracing
Possibility

The first three sections of this book are based on the premise that if you closely and courageously examine a painful, traumatic experience, one that most likely includes some of the most difficult days of your life, this will ultimately serve to lighten the burden that you carry in your heart. This process includes acknowledging the fundamental changes caused by trauma and making space for grieving the life you lived and the person you were before. This requires looking into the abyss of absence and sitting intentionally in the presence of sorrow.

By taking these steps, you ready yourself for the rest of this book, which is about looking forward. In the next four sections, you have the opportunity to explore what's possible, create new dreams for the future, embrace your new self, and begin to live your new life. This work requires a different type of courage than coping with trauma, since it means taking the risk to open your heart again to joy, love, and possibility.

Chapter 14

Opening Your Mind and Your Heart

Enduring an intense, life-altering experience is an accomplishment that deserves acknowledgment and celebration. Please make space, right now, for honoring the tenacity and determination that you have shown in order to arrive in this moment.

You have survived. There is nothing small about this fact.

Surviving requires grit and strength. However, my hope with this book is to help you do more than survive. I want you to tap into and use that power to thrive.

The most common obstacle to living a full and meaningful life is the fear of further pain. As everyone learns eventually, dreams don't come with guarantees. If we didn't realize this before a life-altering trauma, we do afterward, when our disappointment is heartbreaking. After surviving an experience that shatters our life, the idea of creating a different life based on new dreams can feel pointless. Why risk expressing our desires, hopes, and aspirations when doing so might only lead to heartbreak all over again?

After Phil's death, I put my heart on lockdown. Thinking back now, my heart at that time became like a Transformer. Push one button and my regular human heart became a steel-plated, supercool race car that materialized in a flash. Within moments, my Porsche Speedster raced away from whatever emotion threatened to harm me. My Transformer race car was red, of course.

This emotional shutdown applied not only to romantic love, but to all forms of tenderness, excitement, and joy. If an emotion came with the possibility of disappointment, I was not interested. I would even change the TV channel to avoid commercials that were too heartwarming. Nope. Nothing was getting near my heart; of that I was sure. Get too emotionally close to me, and you would hear the distinctive metallic clicks that signaled my metamorphosis into a getaway vehicle.

Sitting in my pain was familiar, even comfortable after a while. I grew accustomed to shutting out disappointment through the illusion of safety that my red Porsche heart provided. It took me years to realize that I wasn't actually shutting out pain or limiting my vulnerability. I was just separating myself from fully experiencing the life that was right in front of me.

Avoiding positive emotions is a subtle and sneaky act of self-protection. We can fool ourselves into thinking that if we never expect anything good to happen, then we won't be surprised or hurt when something awful does happen. When trapped in this way of thinking, we teach ourselves to expect the worst. Rather than hope for the best, we avoid all positive expectations. An emotional lockdown creates a facade of safety, which our broken hearts yearn for. Not feeling anything but pain creates the illusion that no further hurt can be experienced.

When our hearts have been broken, sometimes we fear everything good. We fear lightness and joy. We fear fun and excitement. We fear allowing our hearts to sing. We fear falling in love with someone or allowing someone to fully love us. We fear change and pain and disappointment — because we've lived through all of that already, and our main goal becomes never revisiting that pain.

What about your heart? Have you constructed a fortress around it? If you have, I understand in ways that no words can fully convey. The trouble is that closing down one's heart offers only an illusion of safety. Our hearts can't be safeguarded by avoiding positive emotions, shutting out people we love, or refusing to participate in life by going through the motions of living without truly engaging.

Instead, the armor we think is protecting us from future pain is actually only keeping out the joy while holding on to our current suffering.

In order to release pain, we must open our hearts. We must engage in play. We must try new things. We must love. We must risk the pain of disappointment in order to make way for the incredible gift of possibility.

When we stop allowing fear to direct our path, an endless array of possible directions suddenly appears. In your life, if fear of failure, heartbreak, or ultimate disappointment were not a factor, what would you do? Where would you go? Who would you take with you?

When we welcome possibility, we place ourselves in the flow of creativity. When we open our minds and our hearts to what could be, questions lead to answers, answers lead to action, and action leads to even greater possibility. When we make the powerful decision to start anew, the freedom that comes from accepting our new selves and the confidence we've gained through survival become our most valuable assets.

I know from experience that this is easier to recognize than to accomplish. At first, it can feel impossible to envision a positive future that includes but is not overshadowed by the past. We can convince ourselves that dreams never come true. The evidence of our own traumatic experience is that dreams can turn into nightmares without any notice. The thought of re-creating our lives can feel much scarier than living through what we've already survived. Not only is hope scary, but we might not even know what to hope for. We might wonder, is it even possible to hope when we can't define what we want? How do we hold on to hope if we no longer believe in positive outcomes?

In the first weeks and months after Phil's death, I just hoped that I would survive. I hoped that somehow the experience I was living through would become bearable. I hoped that the sadness I felt every single minute wouldn't overtake me and leave an empty shell in place of the vibrant woman I was before. Each day my hope shifted. Some days I had more hope and some days I had less, but most days my hopeful aspirations didn't extend much past the next twenty-four hours.

As I continued coping with the day-to-day reality of life without Phil, I realized that my hopes were shifting. Slowly, I discovered that I wanted to live. I didn't want my widowhood to be the only experience that shaped the rest of my life. I began to hope that I could develop the courage to care.

The desire for a meaningful life didn't arrive as a fully formed aspiration, but rather as a whisper whenever my interest was piqued by a project or when a friend made me laugh.

Possibility became what I hoped for, though I am not sure I'd have been able to express it that way at the time. Knowing that I wanted a life that was lighter and more fulfilling than the one I was living was enough. Hoping for more was enough: more laughter, more fun, more joy, more friendships, more love, more compassion, more empathy.

We get to choose what we want more of in our life. When we do, hope follows. Once we determine what parts of our current life no longer serve us, they can be let go. That letting go frees up space for new ideas, new passions, and new dreams. It's important to ask yourself the question: What do you want to do, to be, to have more of in your new life? To turn surviving into thriving, do something you've never done before, whatever piques your interest now, or revisit a hobby you once loved. What's whispering to you? What fills your soul? Asking these questions with an open mind and heart encourages a lighthearted exploration of new experiences that may lead to surprising interests and passions.

Keep these questions and any answers that arise in mind as you take the next step in this process: examining your current lifestyle to discover whether the way you are living your life right now supports the evolution of your new self.

Chapter 15

The Making of
an Unexpected Life

As I struggled to adapt to the changes brought on by Phil's death, I often said that the only widowed people I knew personally were my grandmother and my great-aunt, both of whom died before I was widowed. This statement expressed my feeling of being alone in my newly widowed life. I knew no one in my world at that time who shared the experience of outliving a partner. But beneath my feelings of loneliness and my intense desire to find other widowed people was a further truth: I didn't have much respect for my grandmother. I loved her, but she was never a person I admired or wanted to emulate.

My grandfather, John Neff, was a dominating presence. He struggled with alcoholism in his early years, and he credited finding and working the steps of Alcoholics Anonymous (AA) with saving his life. By the time I was born, he had been sober for fifteen years and was a leader in the AA organization. John Neff was a name known both locally and nationally; he sponsored countless people who were struggling with alcohol addiction and spoke at meetings across the United States about the power of the AA process. Tall, solid, direct, magnetic — if you were in a room with him, you knew it.

At the same time, it might take you much longer to notice his dedicated sidekick, Elsie Jayne Neff, known to her family as Jayne and to her grandkids as Grandma Neff. She was a woman completely focused on her husband, who made every decision and directed their lives in ways large and small. One of her regular contributions to their partnership was the creation of handmade matching outfits for them to wear on trips or for special events. She wanted the fact that they were together to be clear.

Grandma Neff was the epitome of a sweet but sassy granny. Mild, unassuming, agreeable, but she would swat you if you were misbehaving within arm's reach. Part of our family lore was that she'd suffered an early trauma to her brain. Grandma would often tell us that she "wasn't quite right" whenever she searched for a word that she couldn't remember, struggled to express her thoughts, or labored while trying to understand a concept being described by someone else.

By the time I was old enough to remember her, she'd also been diagnosed with diabetes. Among the adults, there were frequent discussions about her sugar consumption. She regularly dispatched her grandkids to "Go get Grandma a little sliver of cake." My siblings and I were her sugar dealers, and once we'd handed her the requested treat, she'd wink and take a bite before another adult noticed. Though I remember her "getting a shot" daily, as a child I had no concept of the challenges of living with diabetes. If you'd asked me at the time, I would have told you that Grandpa was in charge of Grandma's health. He administered her insulin, chose her meals, kept an eye on what she was eating, and scolded her for noncompliance.

When I was around twelve, my grandparents began traveling throughout the United States in their RV trailer. They planned their trips based on Grandpa's speaking schedule for AA. True to form, Grandma made them matching jackets with a map of the United States on the back. Whenever they traveled through a new state, she embroidered it with bright colored thread. I can still hear the pride in her voice when she recited the list of states they'd recently explored, pointing to each one on their matching denim jacket travel maps.

John and Jayne spent eight years living in their RV, traveling to whichever state was next on his speaking gig lineup and focused entirely on the life he wanted to lead. Until the day he found a lump in his neck while they were in New Mexico. That discovery changed everything — the mass he found was a sign of advanced-stage lung cancer. They came home and parked the RV in a friend's driveway, and he died just two months later.

At the time, I was twenty years old, newly engaged, and totally clueless about the experience awaiting my grandmother as we stood beside her while her lifelong love was buried. She was dry-eyed, stoic, and firmly attached to my dad. Immediately, she looked to him and my uncle Tom to fill the gap in leadership left by her husband's death.

It wouldn't have surprised me if she had chosen a matching outfit for them to wear at his funeral. At the time of his death, they'd been married for forty-nine years, and for eight of those years, they'd traveled the United States together, living full-time in a trailer with side-by-side armchairs. They had been inseparable, and now she was alone.

Every person who knew Jayne was concerned about how she would live without John. He had taken care of the bills, planned their trips, handled all matters related to their RV, and chosen what they watched and where they went. She had literally been along for the ride. Now she was in the driver's seat, and we were all pretty sure that she didn't know how to drive. In one fell swoop, she had no home, no husband — and her legs weren't long enough to reach the pedals on the truck she owned.

The only thing most people knew about Jayne was that she was married to John. Her story was his story, and most people felt sure that without him she would just wither away. Instead, she marched forward and showed all of us doubters that she could and would create a new life for herself.

The house in which John and Jayne's kids grew up was sold when they hit the road full-time. Jayne wanted to keep their house as a home base, but John didn't agree. His opinion won out. This left her with only the RV as a home when he died, and she had no interest in traveling without him. She wanted to live in the city where she'd spent most of her life and be available for the family events that they'd missed so often when they were on the road. Turns out, she did have preferences, and suddenly she wasn't afraid to make them known.

Step by step, she settled into a different life. First, she moved into a mobile home near my parents' house and made it her own by displaying knickknacks on every surface. She bought a dog for company, made friends with her neighbors, and signed up for painting classes, though more to meet people than to learn how to paint. Her disinterest in the nuance of putting brush to canvas usually ended in her getting tired halfway through a project and enlisting the help of classmates to complete her masterpiece. The fact that she wasn't the sole artist didn't dim her enthusiasm for the process or the results. In time, every room in her home was covered in Jayne Neff original artwork.

One point of contention between Grandma and my dad was her driving. She was a terrible driver, and for at least eight years she hadn't been behind a wheel at all, but she wanted the freedom that driving offered — she had places to go. One of her early purchases was a car that she could drive comfortably, but her lack of practice led to "little accidents" that made her a hazard on the road. At one point she needed to renew her license, but in order to do so she had to pass the driving test.

My dad didn't want Grandma to drive, but he wasn't worried. He felt confident that she wouldn't pass the test to renew her license. After countless attempts, he stopped making himself available to drive her to the Department of Motor Vehicles, assuming that she would eventually give up the campaign to secure a valid license. Not to be foiled, she hired the young man who lived next door as a chauffeur. Then she passed a hundred-dollar bill to the examiner (I imagine she also gave him one of her signature winks) and miraculously passed the test on her twenty-fifth attempt. With her new license in hand, she promptly rear-ended the person in front of her right after leaving the DMV parking lot. She was very annoyed when that collision ended her driving career.

Painting classes, gardening workshops, attending every school play and family event — Grandma was clearly and unexpectedly happy. She learned to pay the bills, managed her diabetes, ran her household, and watched whatever she liked on TV. But the most surprising development in Grandma's remade life was that she began going to church. On purpose.

John Neff was raised in a Catholic/Methodist home. His mother died when he was young, and his older sisters wanted to ensure that her Catholic faith remained a part of her son's life, so they made sure that he attended mass every Sunday. When his father remarried, John's Methodist stepmother required that he attend services with her in addition to going to mass. After years of attending two services every Sunday, John determined that he would not step foot into a church again — and he never did. This of course meant that my grandma, whose early life didn't include a regular religious practice, didn't attend any kind of church, either. As far as we knew, both of my grandparents were actively opposed to organized religion.

The family in which I grew up regularly attended a local church. My mother grew up in the Catholic Church, and eventually my dad found value and a sense of community there as well. The Catholic faith includes rites of passage for children throughout their lives, and though my grandparents would attend the after-party for any religious milestone reached by one of their grandchildren, attending church services was not happening.

After Grandpa died, my dad started inviting Grandma to join the family at church on Sundays as a way to include her in their daily lives. By this time, I was living on my own, and news of Grandma's attendance at mass came to me second-hand. What began as a way to keep busy became a place where Jayne created her own community. Having lived for decades within the social structure created by her husband, she not only flouted his strong beliefs about organized religion but developed her own equally strong sense of belonging within the church community. Her desire to build a life reflective of her new values outweighed any hesitation she may have felt as she crafted a completely different life. She eventually chose to be baptized in the Catholic Church — the same one that my grandfather would not step foot in no matter who was getting baptized or receiving a sacrament.

I will never forget being told by my dad that Grandma was going to be baptized. Um, what? Part of me wondered if she really understood what she was doing. But I also clearly recall her baptism day. She was beaming. She was proud and happy and included. She was in her element.

From then on, Grandma was at the church more often than any of my family members. She worked at the food bank, joined lunch groups, was a regular member of service committees, and attended Bible studies (despite her dyslexia) and crafting groups. She thought God was just fine, but she wasn't that concerned with the religious aspects of church; she was there because she had found her people. This community stayed with her through to the end of her life, eight years after the death of her husband. Grandma packed a lot of living into those years, during which she not only found religion and community but also accessed the power of integration in a way few others I've met have done as effectively.

As I was living my young adult life, welcoming three awesome kids during my first marriage, Grandma Neff was remaking herself, and I didn't even notice.

Then, after Phil died, I traveled the United States for years seeking examples of widowed people who thrived after the death of their partner — but without considering for one moment the only widowed person I had really known. Every time I mentioned Grandma, I did so only to illustrate and express how alone I felt in my widowhood. I told the story of a heartbroken me who was left with "only" her deceased grandmother and great-aunt as examples of widowed life. Up to then, I had never taken the time or made the effort to get to know the new person my grandmother had become, but eventually, I began to realize that my grandmother not only survived being widowed, she actually thrived after the death of the man who had dictated her every choice for almost fifty years. The more I thought about the way she lived her life after a tragic event that many thought might kill her, the more I wondered where she found the strength to remake her life.

To discover the answer to where she found this courage and determination, I revisited her past, and I discovered there was a lot I didn't know about my grandmother. For all the time I'd spent seeking an inspirational woman to model surviving and thriving in widowhood, I had missed the most obvious one.

Twenty years after Grandma's death, a genealogy search conducted on behalf of a man adopted through a convent at birth led to an astonishing discovery. Jayne had become pregnant at fifteen in the late 1940s. At that time, a girl in her situation was often sent to a convent to give birth and then compelled by the adults around her to give the baby up for adoption. No one knows if she was given a choice about the fate of her child, or how she felt about being separated from her family and making her way through an unplanned pregnancy in the company of strangers.

One clue to the emotional and physical stress can be found in what happened just days after her son's birth. The reason Grandma "wasn't quite right" for the rest of her life was that she had suffered a stroke after giving birth at sixteen — in a place far from home to a child she wasn't able to mother.

Her stroke was significant and prohibited her from travel. By the time she was able to return home, she had been away for most of a year. Fast-forward to her seventeenth birthday, and she was married and pregnant with another son. I can only imagine how hard being pregnant again must have been and how much she must have ached for the child she had to give away. Two more children, born only eighteen months apart, then followed.

By the time she was twenty-two, Jayne had suffered a stroke, given birth to four children, and realized that the man she married was an alcoholic.

On Christmas Day four years later, my grandfather took two of their kids with him to pick up a family member for their holiday dinner. Because he was drunk, he got in a single-car accident that hospitalized both boys. Jayne gave John an ultimatum — stop drinking or get divorced. Even now, typing those words causes disbelief. I cannot imagine my grandmother opposing or directing my grandfather in any way. Yet she did just that. She told him to clean up or get out, and she meant it, knowing what a divorce would mean for her. The year was 1954 and divorcées were considered scandalous. She knew that leaving her husband would make her a single mom to three children, and she would have to figure out how to feed and house them, having never held a job in her life. In the end, John chose to get help, and as he settled into recovery, his role as head of the household was cemented for the rest of their lives.

Ten years later life took a tragic turn. Peggy Jayne, their middle child, was diagnosed with a brain tumor. Over the next three years, she had repeated surgeries, had to relearn how to walk and speak three separate times, and suffered through intense treatments as they relentlessly sought a cure. Grandma took on a job to help pay the medical bills, managed the household, and took care of her dying child. Ultimately, Peggy Jayne's life ended at the age of nineteen, two years before I was born.

When my grandfather died, grief was not new to Elsie Jayne Neff. She was already a survivor, and I had no idea. The sweet and sassy granny that I knew had not only experienced teen pregnancies, a stroke with lifelong effects, giving her first child up for adoption, and being married to an alcoholic, but also the severe illness and death of her middle child — all before I took my first breath. Every hardship Jayne endured helped her to survive the next one.

Elsie Jayne dug deep into a well of courage everyone around her doubted. She didn't give up on life when doing so may have seemed easier. She challenged the norms that were standards in her previous life and explored new ideas — creating a community of her own that reflected the new values she espoused.

For almost thirty years I viewed my grandmother's life through the eyes of a child. Her courage and determination didn't become clear to me until I started writing this book. Elsie Jayne Neff's story is her own, and it embodies the power of out-of-the-box thinking in order to rebuild a dismantled life. She embraced her new self wholeheartedly. She allowed herself to evolve — to become a different person after her husband's death. I fell in love with the concept of integration before realizing that my grandma epitomized it. She used the tools she acquired in the past to survive the hardships in her present and to craft a meaningful future.

I wish my grandma were still alive so that I could tell her that I see her now. I am astounded by her tenacity and inspired by her courage. I hope she knows how grateful I am for providing me with such a personal and powerful example of how to live every moment we are gifted.

Chapter 16

Choosing Growth

When you begin to craft a life in the wake of a tragic experience, look for examples of people who've lived through a similar challenge — and thrived. Read their stories. Get to know the hardships they've overcome. Explore these stories through books, videos, or coffee dates. Being introduced to others who have survived the unthinkable personifies hope. If the person you are getting to know can survive a life-altering tragedy — then you can, too. The proof lies in the successful thriving of other people. Hope becomes more than a concept when that powerful feeling of possibility is represented by another human being. When we struggle to believe in our own ability to thrive, we can lean on the reassurance offered by others who have done so. Witnessing another person's evolution makes growth seem possible.

Elsie Jayne Neff's story is one example of a person who re-created her life several times in the wake of an array of traumatic experiences. Every time she was knocked down by life, she stood back up. Each time she was pushed to the brink by a new challenge, she leaned on what past experiences had taught her to survive. My grandma racked up an arsenal of tools for coping with trauma that served her throughout her life, but I never knew it. Grandma Neff was a key example of integration at work.

Jayne lived a simple life. She didn't start a foundation, advance her education, or even complete high school. She didn't build a career or start a movement. Her thriving was personally profound. She was subtly, almost secretly victorious in the face of every obstacle.

The most powerful lessons taught by integration blend into our everyday lives. Integration is a daily practice that will help you build a life that you love, much like my grandmother did. Her evolution played out before my eyes, and I didn't even notice because from the outside she appeared to be just living her daily life. Occasionally, I'd be surprised by reports about how well Grandma was doing. The fact that she was enjoying a season of her life most people assumed would be full of only sadness and longing was often overlooked. But she didn't care who was watching; she continued quietly building a life that mattered to her. That is the whole point of integration, to use the lessons and tools developed through our past experiences to build a life that matters to us.

I'll never know for sure how aware my grandma was of the role her past played in her present or her future as she made her way through the last big challenges of her life. What I do know is that Jayne leaned on everything her varied life experiences taught her as she rebuilt her life. She lived with and through unhappiness, pain, and heartbreak repeatedly. Perhaps her past taught her to make the most of the opportunities before her. The challenges she overcame might have taught her to grasp joy whenever possible. I wish I could ask her. I'd love to listen to her story in her own words, but I suspect she would downplay her courage. She might tell me that she had no choice in each situation but to move forward.

Many people who've lived through trauma have said these words to me as if the outcome of their situation was preordained. I disagree. We always have a choice about how we live our lives. Moving forward with courage through the aftermath of a traumatic event isn't a foregone conclusion; it is exceptionally hard work. We can choose to make the effort that growth requires, or we can choose to shrink into our pain. The power to select our path is ours. Each minute ushers in an opportunity to choose between suffering and evolution. The pendulum of choice will likely swing between shrinking into pain or jumping into growth with a huge variety of experiences in between. The key is remembering that growth is a choice that fosters a slow and steady movement toward hope and renewal.

This opportunity to choose growth every day can be annoying or even heartbreaking. We might be exhausted. Living with trauma has that effect. Since the pain we feel isn't usually something we've chosen, being told that we're responsible to create a new life can make us angry. Especially if we loved our lives before. Every feeling is valid. It's okay to be annoyed, angry, disappointed, and sad. Lean into those feelings and give them space to be processed, experienced, and honored. Then dig into the power of survival and choose to grow. Not all at once, not necessarily in any linear fashion, but in order to create a new life, we must choose to grow.

Remember, we don't have to do it alone — and I hope you won't. Evolution can be a team sport, even when we are each working on our own project. This is the power of survival stories. When someone else's struggles resonate with our own, we can use their evolution as inspiration for ourselves.

While survival stories don't provide an exact navigational map for our healing, the example of another human who has managed to thrive — not in spite of their pain, but because of it — is like discovering a lighthouse in a storm. Our goal isn't to follow the exact route of other boats, but rather to head in the direction of the lighthouse as we make our way through our own storm.

Inspiration can be found in unexpected places. Instead of seeking stories of largesse and grand-scale thriving, look to the people in your own life. Ask yourself what they've lived through. I traveled the world, taking planes, trains, and automobiles to locations near and far, to meet widowed people and to record what they learned as they journeyed through pain and heartbreak. I desperately wanted to meet people who rebuilt meaningful lives. I wanted to know how they managed to take the crumbled pieces of a past life and make something beautiful from them.

I was shocked to discover a powerful example of thriving post-trauma sitting in an armchair watching soap operas in her mobile home surrounded by Jayne Neff & Co. acrylic paintings. My widowed grandmother found a way to become the one thing that no one thought possible after her husband died — happy.

Choosing growth means taking the hard-won lessons of tragedy to rebuild a new self. Like Jayne, each re-creation we live through informs our ability to survive and offers us the opportunity to thrive with new power, new intention, and new focus.

Seek out your lighthouses, follow the light, and choose to craft a life that matters to you.

IMAGINE

Dreaming a New Dream

❦ —— ❧

Dreaming a new dream after living through a life-altering experience requires the courage to acknowledge the pain and heartbreak of disappointment. But rather than using that pain as a justification for avoiding growth, dreaming again uses the pain that changed us as a catalyst for expansion and transformation.

Chapter 17

The Courage to Dream

Dreaming used to come easy. When I was a child, I dreamed of being a teacher. Sharpened pencils made my heart sing, and I loved cleaning the chalkboard erasers at school, prancing outside to bang the felt blocks together while imagining myself at the front of the room leading a class of eager students. When I envisioned my adult life, I didn't even factor in the idea of disappointment. In my youth, everything felt possible.

I realize now how fortunate I was to live in that world of possibility. Not everyone's childhood includes a safe space for dreaming. Not everyone enjoys the sense of security that suggests the world is a place of opportunity. When disappointment early in life crushes youthful ambitions, people can feel that reaching for something wonderful is ridiculous or even dangerous.

Our early relationship with disappointment plays a role in our ability to look into the future with hopefulness. This is a perfect example of how our past shapes our present and our future. If past experiences show that good things are a part of life, we learn to expect good things in the future. If life has included a series of challenges and disappointments, we learn to expect bad things. And when life includes a significant traumatic experience that alters our whole world, both the present and future may look grim through the lens of heartbreak.

Experiencing trauma sometimes leads to a defeatist mentality. Experience tells us that hopes can be crushed and the pain that follows should be avoided. It can be easy to fall into the trap of attempting to avoid disappointment by presupposing that all things will end badly. Making this assumption is like heading pain off at the pass. If we assume the worst and set our sights very low, heartbreak can't sneak up on us. If we believe that we are defeated before we begin, eventual failure is a comfortable and expected outcome.

However, experiences that change our life in positive ways alter the narrative. Consider your own unfolding story. Your childhood and upbringing no doubt contained challenges, failures, accidents, and terrible outcomes, but it almost certainly also included moments of contentment and happiness, successes, and surprising joys. This demonstrates that wonderful things can follow difficult things.

One problem or even a string of hardships doesn't negate the possibility of wonder around the next corner. Every positive experience we live today becomes part of our past tomorrow. Our past narrative is shaped and reshaped day by day. Of course, our lives are bound to include both struggle and triumph. Yet the experiences we let shape us are often the painful ones.

Experiencing trauma changes the way we walk in the world while even our most triumphant successes are less likely to change our daily habits. Pain avoidance is a strong motivator.

Horrible experiences whisper warnings in our ear about possible danger around every corner.

So what do we do about that glimmer of hope that shines under the door we've shut on possibility? When life calls us forward, how do we respond?

Embracing a new dream requires not only courage but the willingness to face heartbreak again — because of course that could happen. Imagine each new dream as a coin in which one side represents beautiful fulfillment and the other ultimate disappointment. These two possibilities flip over and over as we toss the coin in the air. There is no way to know which side of the coin will land faceup. Clearly, life doesn't offer guarantees. Yet we know for sure that sitting safely in our pain will not open the door on what could be.

In an effort to avoid disillusionment, we may squash opportunity — even though each coin toss is equally likely to land on the beautiful fulfillment side. Forgetting that all surprises aren't painful is a common side effect of living through something awful. Once we've experienced crippling pain, we often forget that some life-altering experiences are filled with joy and wonder.

Building a new life will require us to believe in the power of our dreams.

The courage to really embrace and revel in our dreams is vital. Living a dream without truly embracing the wonder of the experience is possible — just as swimming along the surface of a lake but not diving underwater is possible. Yet if we never fully submerge our body, we will never experience the thrill of breaking through the glassy water or the incredible lightness of buoyancy. A dream that lacks the full commitment of our mind, heart, and body will wither. In order to create a new life, we have to believe in the power of what we are creating. That doesn't mean we won't be scared to death, but as John Wayne suggested, we have to saddle up anyway.

One of my most beautiful (and terrifying!) post-trauma dreams arrived in the form of a man living on the other side of the world.

After Phil's death, I knew very early on that I didn't want to live the rest of my life without a partner, even though the idea of loving someone else made me feel physically sick. At first this knowledge just sat in the back of my brain, almost taunting me. Not wanting to be single for the rest of my life was not the same as being ready and willing to participate in a new relationship. I wanted to be able to show up and be present for a new partner, and I couldn't figure out how that was possible. I thought I needed to wait for my heart to be fully healed before I'd be ready to seek new love. What I didn't realize then was that healing and loving and grieving were all part of the same experience.

Three years after Phil's death, I took a chance one lonely evening and created an online dating profile. Clicking the submit button changed my life. Two years later that choice would lead to me marrying a man who lived in Australia, but how that unfolded is a story for another book.

For now, I'd simply like to introduce my husband, Michael, and explain how choosing to love him has been both terribly hard and incredibly easy.

Right from the start, Michael tested my courage in every way. First, he is mortal. That was definitely a liability. Second, he is kind and understanding and funny as hell. This combination was dangerous because not only did he make me laugh, but he thought the fact that I wore my late husband's wedding ring on my right hand was beautiful. Next, when we connected online, he lived far enough away that I could engage peripherally, which gave me a false sense of security regarding how invested I was in our relationship. I kept telling myself that our correspondence was harmless. What could come of emailing with someone who lived on the other side of the Pacific Ocean?

If I were writing a movie screenplay, our eventual wedding would be the end of the story, wrapped up with a pretty bow. But this is real life, and I am a trauma survivor. That trauma didn't disappear when I remarried, and it still emerges from time to time. My last husband died in an accident that involved a car, so you can imagine how many times I've warned Michael to be careful when crossing a street. Yes, he is a grown man, but his safety is a very tender issue in my psyche. My life experience has taught me that sometimes your partner may walk out the door and never come back. Michael has received many panicked phone calls from a wife who is fuming with anger because he forgot to call and say he would be late — because in my trauma-influenced mind, tardy could mean dead.

This is just one example of the many small ways that Phil's death still influences my behavior and affects our everyday lives. The more challenging impact is my regular tendency to protect my heart by not fully engaging in life. This is where things really get tricky. I am a master at convincing myself that as long as I participate in life outwardly, essentially going through the motions, then I'm good. In those moments, I definitely appear to be living that meaningful life about which I teach regularly. The catch is that, when I am afraid, I can still jump into my red Porsche Transformer heart and speed away. This emotional escape hatch is generally associated with my fear of Michael's eventual death, and it often expresses itself when I refuse help or take on too many tasks by myself, as if I don't have a teammate in Michael.

This remains one of my biggest personal challenges. Just before Phil's death, he and I had found a really good balance between independence and interdependence. We were comfortably settled after learning to trust each other and to work together as we built a new life for our blended family. Then he died, and all of that teamwork went out the window. I had to handle every task, decision, and challenge alone. The struggle to manage the life we built without the benefit of the Michele-and-Phil team is still one of my most painful memories. My aversion to living through that experience again has often kept me from allowing Michael to be a full partner in my life. When I am gripped by this particular fear, I'd rather keep Michael out than share my life with a mortal whose eventual death is guaranteed.

Trauma influences everyone in different ways. We each have to face the unique fears associated with the experience we have survived. We must get to know our fear — name it, explore it, feel it, and recognize that fear when it is pretending to be something else, like protection or wisdom. Truly exploring our fears is the first step in building courage. Before we can be brave, we have to know what we are afraid of.

The evolutionary purpose of fear is to promote survival. We are hardwired to react to our fears in order to stay alive. However, our body's reaction to physical danger isn't much different than to emotional fear. If an animal in the wild is injured, their chance of survival rapidly declines. This reality fuels the ongoing value of the fear reaction in mammals. We fear situations that may harm us. Whether the situation we fear presents emotional or physical danger, our minds will compel us to protect ourselves.

Fear is a valuable danger indicator; that's why the fear response has survived in humans for millennia. But problems surface when we respond to all fears in the same way. Developing the ability to identify and examine our fears helps us to respond to each apprehension appropriately. Obviously, a physical danger has to be acted upon quickly, while dealing with emotional danger requires nuance and reflection. Fear has a valuable role to play in decision-making; it just can't be the only factor if we want to live a full life.

Fear left unchecked keeps us from living.

We don't dream when we are afraid. Instead, we go through the motions of living. We convince ourselves we're thriving, when we're still barely surviving, skirting the edges of life and avoiding joy because we're afraid of it, and that fear takes up too much space to allow for anything else. Until we fully commit to the wishes of our heart, they will remain only whispers of possibility.

Being afraid is not the same as living in fear. When we live in fear, we allow the avoidance of pain to be our primary motivator. Being afraid, on the other hand, acknowledges and recognizes the fears that arise when we face certain choices. Whatever we choose, we do so understanding the pain we want to avoid, while also considering risking that pain for other important factors. Being afraid doesn't keep us from reaching for inspiration, joy, and possibility.

In my own life, I fear loving Michael too much because he will die one day. Having outlived one partner, the idea of outliving another is chilling. Every day, I have to make the choice to fully engage in my new life and to love this man who has brought with him unique and beautiful gifts. Fear plays a part in my daily decisions, but more often than not, fear is no longer the determining factor. Understanding that my fears are a part of my survival instinct has helped me to acknowledge them, explore them, and respond to them with respect as I make choices that allow room for grace and goodness to enter my life. Even when I am afraid. This is one of the most powerful lessons I've learned from my trauma.

Fear has a place, but it can't have the only place in my heart.

Take a moment and consider the fears related to whatever traumatic experience you've been through. Then consider the joys and dreams that you hope will define the rest of your life. If you can own and integrate the fears and difficult realities that your trauma has created, they become tools instead of weapons. Rather than hurt you, these hard-won lessons can be used to help shape a positive and hopeful new life. What you have lived through should never be ignored, but that experience is only one part of your story. When you take ownership of any pain, this puts fear in a healthy place. You can then allow yourself to be afraid and still act with courage to embrace goodness and pursue joy.

Owning the lessons taught by trauma builds confidence in our ability to face adversity as we craft a new future. Integrating this knowledge can help us feel capable instead of victimized. That feeling of competence can give us the courage to step into a new life and to fully welcome new dreams.

Chapter 18

Permission Granted

As you reflect on and evaluate the new you who has been born from trauma, give yourself permission to question everything. Do you believe the same things you used to? Have your priorities and values changed? Do you approach life differently now? Do the same hobbies interest you? Are there things you have always wanted to do and have never done, such as paint, draw, or sculpt? Is there a group, club, or community that you've always wanted to join? Give yourself permission to try anything and everything that sparks your interest.

Try things that scare you. Try things that inspire you. Try things that are completely outside of your comfort zone.

Experiment without expectation or reservation and see what happens. You may dislike certain things you thought you would enjoy, but with each trial you learn something new about the reborn person you are becoming. Explore outside of your previous preferences. Maybe you still like the same foods, music, books, and movies, but try others. For instance, if your favorite vacation has always been a weekend trip to Vegas, go somewhere new. Question little things — do you still enjoy being the one to host parties? — and big things: Do you still find your job and career fulfilling? Might other work now fuel your inner fire?

The point of all this questioning isn't necessarily to change every aspect of your life. It's to explore with an open mind to discover what has already been changed by a traumatic experience and what you might want to change in light of it. After surviving tragedy, you need to give yourself permission to develop new priorities and preferences. Questioning everything is the only way to know for sure if the life you used to lead is still a good fit for the person you are today.

Change doesn't have to be dramatic. From the outside, to others, your new life might look a lot like the life you lived before. You might do many of the same things, have the same friends, and go to the same restaurants. But inside, you may feel very different. Recognizing and honoring these differences, inside and out, is an important step toward self-acceptance.

On a good day, accepting change is hard. It can be particularly difficult to swallow after a traumatic experience, since we didn't choose to alter our circumstances or worldview, but events altered them for us in unexpected, unwanted, and painful ways. Further, we often consider any changes that result from a negative experience to be negative, so we resist them. Other people can resist these changes, too. Those we love often don't want us to be changed by what we've gone through any more than we like having been changed.

For instance, as an everyday example, consider someone who used to love horror movies, but after surviving a personal attack finds they can't watch those films anymore. To the person, this inner change may feel punitive. The enjoyable anxiety they experienced before has been replaced by genuine terror and a primal urge to run. Their friends may understand and have sympathy for this understandable reaction, but they might also encourage the person to face their fears and continue watching horror movies as a way to not allow the past to control the present. In larger ways, other people in someone's life may be upset at the changes they see, and their natural inclination can be to encourage or even pressure the person to return to their old self as soon as possible to prove that they've healed. Yet we don't facilitate healing by forcing ourselves to do things that feel wrong just because we used to enjoy them. Attempts to return to our old life won't remove the trauma. No amount of encouragement to "get over it" will result in forward movement. Part of healing from trauma means acknowledging and accepting how we've been affected and integrating those changes into a new version of ourselves.

Does that mean that our hypothetical person will never watch horror movies again? Not necessarily. We are constantly evolving, and our preferences will, too. What we need in the immediate aftermath of a traumatic experience will be different from what we need five or ten years later. This is what we discover if we make exploring our preferences and open-minded questioning a lifelong pursuit.

That doesn't make accepting change easy. We often judge ourselves harshly for the ways we feel changed by trauma. This isn't helped when those we love encourage us to return to our old selves, mourn the loss of the person we used to be, or even criticize us for the ways we are now different. When others highlight or judge what's different about us, this can foster a sense of inferiority, of being broken and needing to be "fixed."

Instead, we must accept and honor change and allow it to guide the evolution of our new selves. Even if the people around us are unable to do the same.

Looking to those we love for support and feedback is normal and often helpful. We need loving support and outside perspectives to help cope with and understand what we are going through. But it is possible that the changes we are experiencing will make the people around us uncomfortable. This discomfort is one of the reasons that iterations of ourselves born through trauma often get a bad rap. We aren't the same, and we don't fit the mold we lived before. When we attempt to return to the exact life we lived before trauma entered our world, it's like trying to put a square peg into a round hole. We need people who will support our growth and not try to halt the evolution that was started by our experience.

Others can offer opinions and support, but ultimately, we are in charge. We must give ourselves permission to explore options, consider new challenges, examine our priorities, and make whatever adaptations we feel are necessary to foster the evolution of our new selves.

Check in with yourself right now. How well do you think you are doing when it comes to accepting change? Among the people in your life, who supports these changes the most and who resists? What new things would you like to explore? Then, whenever you try something new, check in with your body. Consider how you feel. What thoughts does that new experience bring up? What feelings surface? Do you want to do it again? Trial and error followed by more trial and error is the best way to find yourself. You will likely discover that some aspects of yourself haven't changed at all, while others may have changed dramatically. Give yourself a chance to discover new possibilities and potential. Your friends and family may be surprised to discover how much they like the new you, even if you don't watch the same movies.

The only permission needed to evolve into a new version of your amazing self is your own.

Chapter 19

Looking Heartbreak in the Eye

Living through a traumatic experience wipes out naivete. I now think of the time before Phil died as an era of innocence. Those were the days when death was a distant and far-off concern that didn't play any role in my daily life. When Phil died, death became personal.

After someone lives through something they were not sure they would survive, they may become hyper-aware of the fact that some other terrible thing could happen at any moment. Trauma survivors understand on a cellular level that pain will always be a part of life. This reality can cause an intense fear reaction to surface. Remembering the searing pain, and realizing that it could return anytime, sets up that preemptive assumption of future heartbreak or horror. Anyone who has lived through a life-shattering situation is not eager to do so again. This type of fear encourages the building of emotional barriers that appear to protect us from pain but can actually prevent us from truly experiencing joy.

A personal example of this relates to the blended family

Phil and I were creating. We struggled for years to combine six kids with divergent needs, a new marriage, and two significantly different parenting styles. Just when I felt we were figuring out how to be a family, Phil died and the family, life, and future we built fell apart. My takeaway from this experience has been that anything I build could crumble — which is true. That's the rub. My fear isn't unfounded, which makes the desire to protect myself fierce.

When the reality that bad things do happen to everyone becomes personal, we never forget this. Instead, we live with the knowledge that things can change at any moment — with the crash of a car, a violent act, the delivery of a diagnosis, the ring of the phone, or a fall on a slippery sidewalk.

We each have a different reaction to this uncomfortable truth. Some people find this reality liberating — they grab life and live it as fully as possible, making the most of every moment. Others find this truth limiting and live a smaller life, with the hope that if they don't have much to lose, losing what they have won't hurt. Still others find themselves in between, wanting to really live but struggling to let go of the fear of future heartbreak.

That in-between space is where I landed. I knew I wanted a full and meaningful life, but while trying to build that life, I was continually tripping over my fear of losing another future. This struggle crystallized leading up to my wedding with Michael.

He and I wanted to start our lives together with personally crafted promises. One week before our wedding, I still hadn't written any of those promises. As a writer and speaker, I assumed that writing my vows to Michael would be easy. But every time I sat down to write, I got stuck on the words "till death do us part."

Phil and I lived these words, and I lived the pain that came after. I was afraid that, when saying these words again, I'd be transported straight back to the roadside where I watched Phil slowly dying. Writing those words into my vows felt wrong, but leaving them out also felt wrong for reasons I could not articulate. Making matters more complicated was the fact that Michael didn't care. He wasn't worried about the exact words we said. He only wanted to be married at the end of the day. He didn't want to cause me any pain. If I felt that saying certain words hurt, he preferred I didn't say them.

Three days before the wedding, with still no handwritten vows, I told my best friend, Michelle, that I wasn't going to say "it." (Michelle is a founding board member of Soaring Spirits, and those who know us both affectionately call her "double L.")

Michelle was quiet for a moment. Then she said, "Don't you think Michael deserves that promise?"

That question clicked everything into place. Fear was driving my decision, but more importantly, being afraid was keeping me from truly committing to my new life. The reason I didn't want to say the word *death* during our vows was my fear that Michael would die too soon, the same way Phil did, before we had a chance to fully share our lives. This wasn't really about Phil or trying to avoid the mixing of two marriages. Saying the word *death* at our wedding felt somehow like inviting death into our day, almost like I would be asking for it. Five years after being widowed, I was just beginning to discover the ways my lived experience would influence my new marriage. Integration is a lifelong endeavor.

The day of our wedding, on a gorgeous California September afternoon, I did promise to love and honor Michael until death do us part. This vow was made with clear eyes and without a single thought of Phil's death. This promise was made to the man standing in front of me, beaming love. I spoke these traditional words not because I felt obligated or pushed into saying them, but because I realized that these words were a symbol for me of entering into the next phase of my life with my whole self. I didn't want to leave any part of who I am out of the promises I made to Michael that day.

The struggle I experienced with my fear is also a great example of applying fishbowl thinking to a life situation. Michelle and I have lived through the death of both of our husbands. Our widowhood first brought us together, and we've ridden the roller coaster of grief side by side for almost twenty years. She knows me, and she isn't afraid to gently but firmly challenge me when a decision I'm making seems off to her. I consider Michelle a fish feeder. She has supported me through awful times and celebrated with me during awesome times. Which means her opinion matters.

Michelle didn't force or push my decision regarding my vows. She simply asked the question that occurred to her, and I knew my job was to consider seriously what she had to say. That's what the fishbowl guidelines are for: to remind us to listen to people whose opinions we trust, whether or not we agree or choose the course of action that they suggest. The people in your life who fall into this category are vital for helping you see through your fears and make your way through life's challenges, and for reminding you to sing while in the lifeboats. Michelle helped me identify that what I was really afraid of was joy.

Early in my grief I didn't realize that welcoming joy into my life again would require more courage than facing down pain, grief, and hardship. I got used to those challenges. Joy is actually a hell of a lot scarier than pain. Who knew?

Joy still scares me. As the days roll by and August 31, 2005, retreats further into my past, the number of wonderful things that have happened since are revising my narrative about my past. Yes, my husband died in a horrible accident, but I've also discovered new passions, traveled to new places, welcomed new love, and populated my world with people and causes that make my heart sing. As the number of joyful experiences increases, I am aware of the ticking of the clock that counts how many days have passed in which I've been mostly happy. Because my life experience tells me that this can't last. Hardship is coming; it always does.

Being afraid of pain after surviving trauma is reasonable, but avoiding suffering by building emotional barriers won't save us from heartbreak. Distancing ourselves from others only causes a different type of pain, a kind that is avoidable. By disengaging in life to avoid disappointment, we create the hurt we hope to avoid — it's just wearing a different costume. When we choose fear as our main decision-making factor, our life becomes so small that there isn't room for anything but fear.

When used a different way, that same fear can be transformed into a tool. When trepidation or anxiety surfaces, ask yourself what you are afraid of. Look your fear in the eye, acknowledge what you think may happen, and then imagine how you will feel if it does. Take a deep breath and honor that fear, which was born of the life-altering pain that you have already experienced. Then let that fear go and choose to take a risk on life.

Ultimately, fear has become one of the ways I keep myself engaged and present in my daily life. When I'm afraid, I know I am likely getting close to a desire of my heart or a person that I don't want to live without. For me, learning to consistently choose life over fear has taken practice. Sometimes I face down my fear multiple times in a day. Other times I will go weeks or months without being haunted by the specter of pain that I assume is right around the corner. Over and over again, I choose the potential for pain over the certainty of missing out on opportunities that require me to risk in order to gain. Fear has become my reminder to live right now while I have the chance.

On our wedding night, after all the guests went home and the fruitcake was eaten, Michael and I were lying exhausted side by side in our hotel room as tears started streaming down my face.

Michael looked at me with concern and asked why I was crying. As I tried to explain, a flood of tears began in earnest. Reflecting on the day, I realized that until that moment I didn't really believe that he and I would be married. For two years I was terrified that something awful would happen that would prevent us from enjoying the very moment we were living.

Each time that fear surfaced, I faced it down and kept planning the life I wanted. Every time my past experience told me that life doesn't work out the way we plan, I responded that sometimes it does. Each time fear tempted me to make my life small, I remembered a different truth that is also proved by my past: I can do hard things. But until the day was done, the marriage was sealed, and the guests were gone, one little scared part of me didn't believe that goodness was actually as real as hardship.

On my wedding night I cried for the part of me that couldn't believe in joy, and I cried for the part of me that welcomed the joy I feared without knowing how long it will last.

That kind of courage will change your life for the better.

RECLAIM

Rocking Your Phoenix

—⊱———⊰—

Transformation is only possible when we are truly open to evolving. Before anyone else can love a new version of us, we must first fully embrace the person we've become through trauma and integrate the parts of our past that hurt and changed us into our present and our future.

Chapter 20

Letting Go of Pain

When living through the early days of a trauma, the depth of the suffering that we experience can be frightening, but our pain also acts as immediate proof that something significant has happened. The wounds inflicted by our experience reflect the damage caused by what we've survived.

Of course, our heart hurts. We've lived through something awful. A pain response is a natural and normal part of experiencing trauma. Where there is pain, there is injury, and the people around us recognize this. The outward signs of our distress are the first signals to them of our state of mind as we walk through the early days of our experience.

However, if our injuries are not visible from the outside, our ability to express the extent of our suffering is the only reflection of the harm we've sustained.

All trauma survivors live with the invisible emotional damage that accompanies life-altering experiences. These wounds can be difficult to identify, but they are often expressed through depression, anxiety, PTSD, isolation, or emotional avoidance.

A variety of physical manifestations of pain are also common as our brains and hearts wrestle with the aftermath of experiencing trauma. Pain becomes a daily constant in our lives. A recurring ache may even serve as a reminder that we are alive, that we did survive.

That is what happened for me. Pain became my friend; I liked that guy a lot. Somehow, I decided that being in pain was a way of recognizing that I was alive and confirming that my love for Phil hadn't died with him. The constant ache kept me going day after day. It was like touching a bruise on one's leg to check and see if the injury, and the limb itself, is still there — poke, prod, repeat.

Every time I connected with the pain of Phil's death, I felt alive. I spent so much of my time feeling numb and dead inside that feeling something was better than feeling nothing, even if that something was pain. This became my norm. What I didn't realize was that by assuming that remembering and suffering were the same thing, I had to keep choosing suffering in order to hold on to everything I had shared with Phil. I developed an unhealthy relationship with pain that was encouraged by the common assumption that in order to heal we have to forget.

There was no way to forget Phil or the life we shared, and if healing meant having to do so, I wasn't interested.

Another complicating factor as I worked through my relationship with pain was the notion that emotional healing happens along a linear path and in a predictable pattern. People around me reinforced this with their concern for and questions about my welfare:

"Do you feel better today than yesterday?"

"Does your heart ache less?"

"Are you thinking more clearly?"

The implication is that suffering should continually decrease over time and that feeling no pain equals full healing.

Yet recovering from trauma and emotional pain is not a linear, sequential experience, in which each day is progressively better than the next. Healing isn't measured solely by rating our daily misery levels. In reality, mending our emotional wounds happens in fits and starts. It is common to experience setbacks in the form of flashbacks, nightmares, struggles with anxiety, and recurring fear. The healing process is unpredictable, with no consistent measures of progress.

At first many survivors are encouraged to express their heartbreak. People want to understand what occurred and how the person they love has been affected. But all too soon the script is flipped and the pressure to heal as quickly as possible often begins. Others can assume that pain will gradually lessen as life appears to return to normal and the horrible experience becomes a thing of the past. Survivors themselves often seek to forget. Why would anyone want to hold on to the pain inflicted by trauma? Shouldn't forgetting be the goal?

In fact, even if it were possible, completely forgetting might often feel worse. No one wants to forget a loved one who has died, nor their lives before tragedy changed their circumstances, such as suffering an injury that now limits their mobility. A person doesn't want to forget who they were and what they loved before a life-altering experience; they want to forget the pain of losing who they were and what they loved.

But we can't outrun unwanted change, and the past doesn't just go away, no matter how much we may wish it would. When we treat healing and forgetting as the same thing, then we make healing as impossible as forgetting. Our every life experience lives in our cells. Try as we might, we can't forget what we've lived through.

Instead, we can seek to make peace with tragic experiences. We can release the pain while acknowledging what's changed and valuing the tools and resources born out of survival. Perhaps counterintuitively, if we recognize and acknowledge the impact of a traumatic experience and how it has reshaped our identity, and as we integrate traumatic events into our new sense of self, this helps lessen the pain over time. This doesn't mean we have to think about what occurred every day. It simply means accepting that everything that happens to us, both the horrible and the beautiful, forms who we are, and so all events deserve to be remembered and recognized. This is how we access the power found in living through heartbreak.

I've met many trauma survivors who struggle to reconcile their need to honor their courage as a survivor of tragedy with their desire to return to a previous version of themselves. They regard the personal changes they've experienced as unwanted, negative side effects of trauma. This results in a painful impasse: trying to remember only what feels positive about a traumatic event while trying to deny what is unwanted.

Still others reflect what I experienced, which is the fear that letting go of pain would mean forgetting what happened. However, whether we like it or not, our hearts will always bear the scars left behind by trauma. We can't undo what's changed or forget what happened. But we can ease our suffering through the hard work of integration. As we process trauma, our pain will eventually decrease. Healing occurs not just because time passes but as a direct result of our efforts to understand our experience and embrace what's changed.

This can be an ambivalent experience. To accept our new selves and any easing of our heartache can seem to lessen the impact of what we've survived. Also, if we allow ourselves to appreciate the initially unwanted personal changes in our perspective, personality, and life, that can feel like we are somehow valuing the tragedy itself. In other words, we can wonder, if something positive develops as a result of something awful, does that make the bad thing good?

It does not. Healing from tragedy, and loving our changed selves, does not mean we value the tragedy. Letting go of pain doesn't mean we will forget what happened, nor does it diminish what happened. Mending heart, body, and spirit requires the courage, determination, and willingness to choose to remember, accept what now is, and process and release the pain so we can embrace our new lives.

What keeps so many of us married to our suffering? Wearing our heartbreak like old slippers can be terribly tempting. The familiar ache that becomes a part of every day is often confused with validation or even love. If we buy into the theory that healing and forgetting are the same thing, then we either hold on to pain as proof of our love or bury our trauma in the backyard of our past, hoping (in vain) that it will be permanently forgotten. In both cases, fear very likely plays a critical role.

Take a few moments to consider your own situation. Do you fear or resist letting go of pain? If so, what would happen if you weren't miserable? Whose judgment do you fear? Do you worry that others will assume that you've forgotten what happened? Imagine not struggling with emotional pain every day: What feelings would replace misery? Are you ambivalent about being seen as a survivor, someone who has successfully created a different life after trauma? Or do you try to escape pain by living as if the event never happened?

You don't need to know the answers to all these questions right now. It's okay to be unsure. What's important is exploring your relationship with pain and identifying whether you have an unhealthy attachment or aversion to heartache. This is critical to your ability — and willingness — to heal. The first step is asking yourself what you fear.

Imagine pain as a huge block of cement that you are holding in your hands. The block is heavy and coarse. Your arms ache from the effort of keeping this block elevated. There is no room for anything else in your hands or in your mind. Keeping this block off the ground is your only focus.

Now imagine setting the block down. All at once, you have nothing in your hands. The freedom will be odd at first because you've become accustomed to the weight you've carried for so long. You may feel empty or unfocused without the ever-present need to manage that block. But in time, as you get used to the emptiness, you may find that lightness follows. Without the persistent need to concentrate on keeping that block aloft, you may find that you have time and energy for other pursuits. Emptiness becomes freedom if we have the courage to release things that do not serve us.

Of course, letting go of pain is not as easy as putting down a cement block and walking away. If it were, there'd be a lot less heartache in the world. Facing fears and traumas in order to understand the changes those experiences have caused is scary and difficult. We release pain once and then find that the cement block we had put down is unexpectedly back in our arms. When we believe that the only way to stop feeling pain is to forget what has happened, life invariably reminds us and the pain of our trauma resurfaces. Sometimes we may fear that no longer feeling pain will mean that we have forgotten what we lost or the people we love. This fear may make us unwilling to release our pain or cause us to revisit the pain repeatedly to confirm that we still remember.

Facing fear and integrating trauma requires practice and repetition. The pain we release is rarely gone for good. At times, past trauma will be stirred by a current experience, and we will revisit that trauma, whether we want to or not.

This is why healing and grieving (and loving) are not linear experiences, and why forgetting trauma isn't possible. Our bodies, hearts, and souls remember the pain of the past as a method for future survival. When a new life experience reminds us of something we've survived, the old pain can resurface and need attention. The good news is that when we've mended the wounds left by trauma once, we know how to do so again. We have already developed the tools to facilitate healing.

Developing the ability to address past hurts and continuing to integrate new wounds into our life is proof that we are healing, which is not an end state but a process. Each time we face trauma and release pain, we build confidence in our ability to manage the next challenge.

You can choose to view your survival as proof of your healing. You can choose to honor the pain you've lived through while allowing your heart to heal. You can choose to remember every type of experience without giving them undue influence over your life. You can choose to ignore the comments made by people who haven't lived through what you have. You can choose to regard the tools, abilities, and perspectives you've gained by surviving trauma as the ultimate expression of that event's significance. You can choose to acknowledge your strength, even though it is a direct result of the pain you've lived through. You can write your own narrative.

Not only can you both remember and heal, but you must remember to heal. Releasing the pain that is connected to your experience will create the space necessary to welcome new emotions, adventures, and people into your life.

Your empty hands will be free to accept new gifts.

Chapter 21

Timing My Marathon

Sometimes the gifts we welcome will come many years later and in unexpected packages.

My second date with Phil involved riding a bike beside him while he completed a twenty-mile training run in preparation for the 2000 Los Angeles Marathon. As we headed out early that morning (with me carrying supplies like a Sherpa), I imagined all the talking we could do over twenty miles of road. I was full of questions about Phil's past and decided this would be a great time to ask about his past relationships. He laughed out loud and said, "I can't talk while I am running." Which was a lie, as we would discover later.

Running became a foundational part of our relationship. We loved running together, especially after Phil learned that he could talk and run at the same time. One of our favorite ways to explore a new city was on foot, jogging side by side. We ran up a variety of mountains, through all kinds of neighborhoods, and over a lot of pavement during our marriage.

As we covered all those miles, Phil and I developed a plan

for me to run my first marathon the year I turned forty, with him playing the Sherpa role for me. If I was going to run 26.2 miles, I wanted some beautiful scenery, so I chose the Honolulu Marathon as my target. We spent a lot of time dreaming about and planning this long-distance run even though my fortieth birthday was years away. Then after Phil died, I mostly forgot about that far-off goal.

However, I continued to run, which became a key coping strategy as I grieved. Though the miles were lonely, jogging through our neighborhood was one of the places I most regularly felt Phil's presence. I could imagine him beside me, offering coaching tips and encouraging me to pick up the pace. A few years later, as my fortieth birthday approached, friends and family began asking me what I wanted to do to celebrate. Many people might consider a nice party or a relaxing trip, but I wondered if I should try to run a marathon without Phil.

This was another instance where I convinced myself that I had something to prove. The goal of completing a marathon had always been mine, but Phil's encouragement and belief in me made covering 26.2 miles on foot seem possible. If I were to abandon a long-held goal that I'd shared with many people in my life, would that be giving up? I couldn't bring myself to say that I didn't want to run a fortieth-birthday marathon without Phil because, in my mind, that meant grief would win. In order to conquer grief, I needed to run a marathon.

Marathon training generally takes six to nine months, depending on someone's physical conditioning. I decided to follow a twenty-two-week training plan, and I targeted the 2009 Los Angeles Marathon. Rather than travel to Hawaii without Phil, I chose to run the same marathon he did. I signed up, paid the fee, and told myself that there was no turning back.

Then I started training. The early training runs were good.

I felt calm and confident as I covered more miles than usual. I used my time to chat with Phil in my head and to dream about the big day when I would proudly cross the marathon's finish line. In my fertile imagination, I even heard the Vangelis theme song from the movie *Chariots of Fire* blaring in my ears as tears of accomplishment streamed down my face. Then training got real.

As my mileage increased, the logistics of running longer than I'd ever run before became complicated. I stashed water bottles along my route to be sure I stayed hydrated, planned circular training courses so I wasn't too far from help if I needed it, and shared my route map with a friend each time I went for a long run. I spent almost as much time planning and preparing as I did covering the miles. As my weekly mileage crept up, my exhaustion level did, too. I became drained and irritable from all of this training on top of working two jobs, caring for my kids, and managing my grief. Running stopped being a respite and started feeling like just another task on my list of things to do.

One particularly beautiful Saturday morning, I headed out for an eighteen-mile run. The planned course was the longest I'd ever attempted and would take me through three different cities. I was nervous and tired and lonely but still determined to prove that I could run a marathon on my own.

The early part of the morning went well. I covered the first nine miles feeling strong and enjoying the perfect weather. When I hit the turnaround point on the route, the realization hit me that I would need to cover all of those miles and make my way back through those three cities — and suddenly home felt very far away. Tears threatened and I struggled to keep my feelings of overwhelm at bay. The only way home was on my feet, so I kept running. My legs cramped, my water got low, the heat increased, and my misery level climbed. As each mile passed, I considered my motives and asked myself who would care if I didn't run this marathon. The only person I was trying to prove anything to was me.

By the time I reached our driveway, I had made my decision. I didn't have to torture myself or run through tears or turn a physical outlet I loved into a chore. I could choose to do what was best for me — today's me.

That was the end of my marathon training. I watched the 2009 Los Angeles Marathon on TV feeling terribly grateful for my soft couch and warm robe.

I thought that was the end of the story, but I was wrong.

During our marriage, Phil and I took all six of our kids on various 5K runs. We chose races in unique locations or those that included activities for kids, but no matter how exciting any race theme or feature might be, our kids complained incessantly. The idea of 5Ks as a family was usually far more pleasant than the reality of dragging a collection of reluctant youths along a three-mile course as they peppered us with questions about how much farther they had to go and when they could get a hot chocolate.

The first Thanksgiving after Phil's death, I thought completing a Turkey Trot 5K as a family in his honor would be a good start to what I knew would be a hard day. Not a good idea. Instead of two adults pushing and cajoling six cranky children, it was just me demanding that the five kids who were with me that day keep moving. Yep, a great way to start the Thanksgiving holiday. I vowed never to take kids on a 5K course again.

Fast-forward eight years later: I was chatting with my daughter Caitlin (then twenty-two and happily living on her own) during our regular morning phone call when she mentioned that she had started running. My first response was to wonder if she was running on purpose. As a child, she was one of the most dedicated anti-5K complainers due to an issue with her knee, and I could not imagine her freely choosing to run anywhere. Turned out, she had come to love the same things about running that I do, and she had begun a regular running routine. Eventually, she invited me to join her for the first 5K that she signed up for on her own. I'll never forget running alongside the Santa Monica pier, chatting as we easily covered three miles side by side. She was a natural, and I could feel Phil beaming.

One race led to the next, and before I knew it, she and I were lined up at the start of a half-marathon in the city of Temecula, which would pass through the vineyards of a little-known California wine region. On a gorgeous fall day, as we waited for the start gun to sound, Caitlin said, "Mom, maybe I should have told you that this run is rated four out of five on the difficulty scale." She chuckled as the mass of people around us started the grueling 13.1-mile run. I didn't mind, since I was in the company of a cheerful young woman who only ten years before believed that I could just get the car and pick her up instead of completing a 5K course.

Over the course of about a year, Caitlin and I completed each of the usual run lengths that lead up to a marathon. With a 5K, 10K, 15K, and more than one half-marathon under our belts, the writing on the wall was clear — we were heading toward a marathon. My suspicions were confirmed on Mother's Day in 2015 when Caitlin gifted me a registration to the California Marathon held in Sacramento, California. My marathon dream was revived.

We started our training six years after I had released myself from the goal of completing a marathon. This time everything was different. I was happily remarried to a man who supported my goals, I was working one job instead of two, and I wasn't raising three teenagers. The training miles were still painful, but in the company of my daughter, they were also joyful. Our good-natured complaints were part of the fun, and I leaned into everything that Phil taught me about distance running to support Caitlin and myself as we covered the miles that would lead us to our shared goal.

On a chilly Northern California morning, Caitlin and I stood side by side in the company of thousands of other runners. Throughout the 26.2-mile journey, we laughed, we cried, we reminisced about Phil — giggling as we wondered aloud what he would think of our pace. Both of us experienced a moment when we thought for sure we would not make it, and we leaned on each other for reassurance that we could. The final three miles were a unique kind of torture, but we held hands as we crossed the finish line. I was so wrapped up in the moment that I forgot to listen for the triumphant sound of *Chariots of Fire*.

Hours later, as we ate all the pizza we could stomach and toasted each other with the cold beers we'd been dreaming about since mile twenty, I was overcome by the fact that my goal had been achieved. Not as a milestone to mark my fortieth year. Not with Phil running beside me. Not on a beautiful island. Not in any of the ways I'd planned or imagined. Everything about achieving this goal was different, and perfectly beautiful.

Deciding to end my marathon training in 2009 made room for the experience I had years later. Instead of forcing myself to stick to a goal I set with Phil, I recognized that my life was different, I was different, and our old shared goal was not a good fit for the new me.

At the time, I felt like I was choosing to never run a marathon. I didn't realize that life might actually offer me another opportunity to meet that goal in a beautiful and unexpected way.

Reflect on any goals, promises, or dreams you have had to release because of what you've been through. Are there goals you still cling to even though you know they do not fit or serve you anymore? Be true to your new self. Acknowledge the fundamental differences in your circumstances caused by trauma. Allow what you have learned to change you, even if this means letting go of things you once treasured. Trust that by letting go you are making space for new, unexpected joys to come, ones that may seem as foreign and unlikely to you as running a marathon with my daughter was to me. After all, I had to offer Caitlin a piggyback ride to the car after our ill-fated Thanksgiving Day Turkey Trot.

Some of the goals, relationships, and dreams that you release may come back to you in a new form, in ways you would never dream of. My marathon was perfectly timed. In 2015, every version of myself was filled with pride as I crossed that finish line in the company of my girl. Together, mother and daughter had both grown into women who could run a marathon.

Chapter 22

Embracing the New You

I haven't always been proud of all the iterations of me. For a long time, I actively despised the version of myself that was born on the day Phil died. My disdain was based on the fact that this me was connected to a trauma that changed the course of my life and took me kicking and screaming in a direction that I didn't want to go. I blamed this version of me for every bad thing that followed Phil's death. Each new challenge I had to face was somehow her fault. Every time she couldn't meet the expectations of the people around her, I imagined how much better my past self would have managed. Her birth was inexorably tied to the most painful time in my life, and I couldn't separate who I was becoming from the trauma that had caused these changes and forced me to adapt.

The irony of my self-contempt was that this new me accomplished quite a lot: I worked two jobs while raising three teenagers on my own, traveled the United States on weekends interviewing thirty widows about their grief experiences, founded an organization that would ultimately provide programming for millions of other widowed people, and maintained life-affirming family connections and friendships that required the ability to step outside of myself in service to others. Yet at the time I would have given anything to have the old me back — the "good" one.

No achievement would have been enough to convince me of my new self's value. I had to keep demonstrating to myself over and over again that I was still capable and deserving of self-acceptance. Compliments and recognition from others didn't matter. I assumed that the people around me were biased. If they really knew how significantly different the new me was to the old me, they wouldn't like her, either. I was damaged goods, and I was just making the best of what was left over from the person I was before.

Ultimately, my disregard for the person I was becoming just made healing that much harder, and overcoming this was one of my biggest challenges. Creating a new and meaningful life is not possible if we hate ourselves. We need to cultivate self-love and self-acceptance. Viewing ourselves as just "okay" won't facilitate healing. We have to honor the person who has survived a life-changing traumatic experience. We have to celebrate that person. Stand in awe of that person. Treat that person like a rock star. We must recognize that a new person was born through trauma and that this person has experienced extreme pain and hardship. Accepting and welcoming our new self is part of how we integrate the turmoil and pain we've survived in order to build a new, satisfying life.

Until we honor this new post-trauma self, our achievements won't matter to us. Kudos won't matter. Other people's opinions won't matter. If we don't embrace the new self that has been birthed through trauma, it won't matter whether or when others embrace us. Others might confirm our worth and value, they might shower us with love and admiration for surviving and adapting to what we've experienced, but if we aren't in touch with our own value, if we reject this powerful message, then we will dismiss the help and encouragement other people are offering.

Affirmations for the New You

Do you struggle with honoring and embracing yourself — particularly the new you who has been scarred and changed by trauma? If so, start by acknowledging your survival. Every difficult step forward you've made ever since that event has been taken by you. You have walked over the burning coals of a life-altering experience and come out on the other side. Yes, you have scars. Yes, you are different in some ways. Yes, you see the world through new lenses. But you have held your life together despite what you have experienced. You have persisted against all odds.

This New You Is a Badass

Your new self was born in distress and agony. At first, right after the painful event, all your energy was consumed with attending to what happened and its aftermath. Along the way, as you've met the daily challenges you've faced, you have learned necessary survival skills that will always stay with you. You have had to be tough to make it this far.

This New You Has Different Strengths

It's vital to acknowledge that who you are in the immediate aftermath of trauma is not who you will become as you heal from the physical, emotional, and psychological impacts of what happened. The new you will be more than a collection of trauma responses. As your recovery continues, your pain, fear, exhaustion, and struggle will eventually lessen — not all at once, and not in a linear progression, but over time — and the new strengths and tools you have developed can be used to fashion a new, positive life.

This New You Has Endless Potential

It's important to recognize that surviving and healing are choices. In order to thrive — by accessing the potential of the new you — you must give yourself permission to thrive and then keep making that choice. Only by truly accepting the new person you have become can you develop the self-esteem and self-confidence to reengage with life and the people you love, fostering the relationships that fill your soul. Until you fully love yourself, you can't fully experience the love of others.

After Self-Acceptance Comes Integration

Once we have made it this far in our recovery from trauma — so that we accept and embrace our new selves — we are ready to tackle integration. That is, we turn our eyes to what can be and use all of who we are and have become to refashion our lives to fit our new selves. Reaching this point requires all the steps this book has discussed so far.

To begin, we have to acknowledge that we have been changed by a traumatic experience and give ourselves time to mourn the self we used to be. We have to take stock of what no longer fits our new selves and identify the people we can rely on, and need to listen to, within our support network. We need to spend time getting to know our new self by testing and examining our previous preferences and priorities. This means choosing to grow and giving ourselves permission to change and dream again. Over time, these steps allow us to understand how a traumatic experience has impacted us, what it has taught us, and how we must adapt, grow, and evolve going forward. This hard work involves weaving the tragedy we've experienced into our daily lives in countless ways, large and small. We might want to forget that the tragedy ever happened, but since that's not possible, or healthy, we must find ways to heal our pain while adjusting to the new realities we now face. When, eventually, we allow ourselves to let go of pain and to embrace our new selves, we give our hearts space for something other than heartache to grow.

That something will be the fruits of integration.

During integration, one of the surprises we discover is that our old self isn't really gone. While we can no longer live the life we did before, we aren't really two people. We have access to everything we knew before, to all our previous talents and skills. All of our previous experience exists inside, in our very cells, and integration uses everything we have experienced to expand our identity and evolve into a new version of ourselves. After trauma, we don't become less; we have the chance to become more.

By accepting the new self that emerges after each challenge we overcome, our coping tools, healing strategies, and sense of resilience grow exponentially. This allows us to craft an even more meaningful life, one with more of whatever we decide is important to us — more kindness, more compassion, more thoughtfulness, more risk-taking moxie, more awareness of the shortness of life. There is no "less than" if we choose to embrace our new selves because then we accept and honor all of who we are.

Evolving into a new self is not like outgrowing an old sweater that must be given away or thrown out. Instead, we weave the old fibers with new yarn to make a new sweater that fits better. This way, we maintain the integrity of our whole selves while adding color and texture, experience by experience.

Integration is not without challenges. For instance, just because we welcome and embrace these changes in ourselves doesn't mean everyone else will. Some people may be scared or saddened by our new self and yearn for the old version, one they miss or find more comfortable. Part of the work of integration is learning to stand proudly in our new identity, no matter how others react.

Ultimately, the only opinion that matters is your own. At the end of every day, you have to like the person that you see in the mirror. Whatever that person has been through, they deserve love and respect for carrying you this far.

Each iteration of your life holds unique gifts, and through integration you get to keep them all. You are the one who gets to choose.

OWN

Let Them
See You Rise

⊱ —— ⊰

The legend of the phoenix describes a spectacularly beautiful bird that engages in a regular cycle of death and rebirth. This makes the perfect metaphor for living through trauma. Tragic events cause the death of one version of ourselves, and from the ashes of our previous life, a new self is born, one rich with possibility. Standing in our hard-won potential, rising from the ashes of one life and opening our heart to the next, is an act of defiant courage.

Chapter 23

When You Are Better After

Living through a traumatic experience often alters our perspective in a way that makes us better partners, employees, leaders, family members, and ultimately, better people.

This truth can be disturbing. Many people struggle to accept anything positive that is born from their experience. I resisted this at first, and I believe the difficulty arises from the fact that we don't want to acknowledge any positive outcomes from tragedy, which can feel like tacit approval or acceptance of the trauma itself.

The story I tell of purchasing a Mini Cooper after Phil's death (see pages 87–90) is a prime example. The fact that this car was associated with Phil's death robbed any joy from my purchase. As ridiculous as it sounds, I didn't want anyone to assume that I preferred a sports car to my husband. Every time someone complimented my car, I assured them that I didn't like it that much. In fact, I often drove our old Explorer just to avoid any conversations about my new red sports car. Other people's excitement inevitably activated my fear that by showing enthusiasm about my purchase I might be sending the message that, even though my husband was dead, I was happy. I didn't want anyone to think that even one part of my life was improved by Phil's death. Nothing good could be associated with the accident that killed him.

This same dynamic can arise if someone receives a large life insurance or cash settlement after their tragic experience. They may struggle with the fact that tragedy was followed by abundance and with the questions, comments, and assumptions of others, who can convey the message, explicitly or implicitly, that someone's tragedy must not be too bad, or maybe was even worth the pain, if their bottom line increased.

If we buy into the idea that positive experiences, life changes, or shifts in perspective that occur post-trauma are wrong, inappropriate, or signal approval of tragedy, our natural reaction is to reject those gifts on principle. Accepting bounty from trauma can feel a bit like accepting an apple from Snow White's evil queen. The offering may feel tainted or dirty.

This is a false narrative. Tragic events remain tragic no matter what good arises afterward. This is particularly true when, because of our experiences, we learn to cope and survive in new ways that improve our lives. As I learned, rejecting whatever joy or fun I might have felt about my new car did not have the effect I'd hoped. No matter what I did or didn't do, this didn't change the opinions of others. People were going to think whatever they wanted about how I was living my life post-trauma, whether I stayed up all night worrying about it or not. The only person hurt by my refusal to enjoy anything, including my long-awaited new car, was me.

Yet I was so busy ensuring that no one thought I could ever be happy again — in order to prove my eternal love for Phil — that I rejected any satisfaction or enjoyment I experienced. I chose pain over joy out of fear that it was wrong for Phil's death to result in any positive impacts on my life.

As this book shows, surviving trauma often leads to personal growth, but this can be hard to accept and embrace. We didn't ask to be changed, and during our rebirth in the aftermath of a tragic experience, we may not want to accept that healing and recovery have made us stronger, more resilient versions of ourselves. We may hesitate to celebrate this growth, since the changes are rooted in trauma and pain. We can struggle to reconcile the good with the bad.

Our willingness to accept the gains that emerge from trauma depends on the story we tell. Not only to others, but to ourselves. What narrative will you adopt?

You can choose to see your evolution as a triumphant reflection of resilience, courage, and survival. You can present your life as a story of redemption in the face of extreme challenges. Or you can tell a tragic tale in which recovery is impossible. In this narrative, honoring the pain of loss and the injuries you've suffered means rejecting any goodness, grace, or benefit.

After Phil died, I chose the second narrative. Rewriting this story became part of my healing. I needed to learn for myself that rejecting happiness would not change the ache I felt every day. I also needed to discover through trial and error that living my life to please others was futile. I could not influence or control how others reacted to whatever I did. In the end, I found that living a tragic storyline only sustained my trauma and limited my ability to heal.

Also, no matter what I did, Phil remained dead and he wasn't coming back. That fact was never going to change, and it would always be part of me. My life wasn't returning to the way it was before, and I realized, instead of holding on to the pain of grief, I needed to focus on growth, recovery, and rebuilding a joyful life.

Will you choose to accept only the horrible parts of your experience, or will you allow space in your heart for positive experiences? Will you accept the good with the bad? The bad is a given; the good is optional.

I am a better person today than I was on the day Phil died. I am a better wife to Michael because of the lessons Phil's death taught me. I am a better mother, friend, sister, and daughter — not because of my trauma, but because I allowed that trauma to change me. I have learned to accept the unexpected gifts that evolution through trauma has brought, and even learned to celebrate them.

I celebrate the blessings that have come from my beautiful husband's death because rejecting the good won't bring him back. Rejecting the tools I've developed and the traits I've discovered won't change the traumas that are a part of my history. Choosing pain over joy won't lessen my heartache. Instead, by owning the whole of my story, I cement my love for Phil into the future I am building. Integration allows me to continue Phil's story, our story, my story without interruption.

You are the only person who can decide whether you will reject or celebrate the beneficial outcomes you've worked so hard to discover. Being a better person after what you've survived is a testament to every version of you — each more beautiful and powerful than the last.

Chapter 24

Own Your Phoenix

Rediscovery is hard work. Your personality, your lived experiences, your past, and your present all play a role in how, when, and if you welcome your new self into the life you are leading today. Every person will experience and integrate these steps in their own unique way. Accepting the opportunities this new self represents can't be forced or rushed. It doesn't matter how long it takes. Give yourself the space you need.

You, in all your imperfect glory, are the most crucial part of this process. No one else can free you from grief, trauma, or fear. You are the one who can and must take the steps to claim and value the new self born through tragedy.

Pay attention to today's version of you — this trauma-influenced self. They are like a trail marker pointing you in the right direction. This self is like a companion who has been walking with you every single day — managing your life, coping with unexpected problems, carrying your books, doing your laundry, keeping you safe, and secretly hoping to be seen by the only person whose opinion really matters — yours.

This is the path of self-acceptance, and no one can walk it but you. There will be bumps along the way. At times, you may wish to return to the former version of yourself. At times, others may wish you were more like the former version of yourself. It's okay. Everyone, including you, needs time to adapt to this new version of you.

Because you know you can't go back to the life you lived or the person you were before.

Roadblocks, detours, and wrong turns are part of every journey. Don't beat yourself up if you arrive at a dead end. Just turn your car around and head in a new direction.

Day by day, you will have new chances to engage in integration and to uncover inspiration. Planning for a life you don't want can feel pointless, but if you keep making the effort to value your new self and access the tools you've acquired through your survival, building a life of meaning begins to matter. One day, you will look yourself in the eye and like what you see, and then crafting your future can even become joyful. I promise.

The new life I've built for myself is a far cry from the one I lived with Phil. I run less, I sleep more. I spend more time with friends. I speak publicly about experiences that my old self hadn't lived. I view the world through a multifaceted lens. My husband is different, my home is different, my family situation is different. I'm happy and proud of the life I've built. Just as importantly, I'm no longer ashamed to be happy. I no longer believe the narrative that a lack of joy is the only way to honor and validate my pain and trauma.

The beauty of integration is that it embraces our whole lives. No version of ourselves is ever lost. Integration helps us to weave all of who we've been into our current selves — physically, emotionally, and mentally. No part is left behind, forgotten, or discarded. We embrace all the skills and perspective we've developed over our lifetime — and this includes what we've learned and how we've been changed by trauma.

As you gain the courage and the confidence to claim the person you've become, your desire to truly live will rise. Answering the call to embody a new life requires courage — precisely because you know that your new life could come crashing down around you at any moment. Having experienced trauma at least once, you know that it is possible, even likely, again. But you also know that, having survived trauma once, you can survive again. In life, the good and the bad always sit side by side. Pain and joy, grief and love, life and death — we can't know one without the other. Joy sits on the other side of pain — this is why, when we avoid pain at all costs, the price is often our happiness, joy, and contentment. Allow yourself to revel in the good, and know that the skills you've gained and the lessons you've learned will carry you through whatever challenges lie ahead. You can trust yourself with your future.

As you pursue integration in your life, and follow the process in this book, try to avoid judging your efforts or holding yourself to impossible standards. Please treat yourself with the same kindness you'd offer your best friend. Do your best to offer yourself grace as you process your trauma. Try to acknowledge the hardships you have already survived.

Are you able to feel sympathy, compassion, and love for your new self? Are you able to embrace the changes that your traumatic experience has caused? Are you ready to let go of pain and to use the tools and strengths earned through surviving your tragedy to rebuild your life?

I hope that reading this book helps you understand, appreciate, and value your new self. I hope it helps make this new version of you feel real. I hope it helps you embrace tragedy as part of healing, rather than reject your experience or pretend it hasn't changed you. I hope that you are ready to let go of pain and chart a new course for your future that honors and values your past, embraces the person you are today, and welcomes the possibility of continued personal evolution.

What if you don't feel ready? What if you can't yet value this new you? What if you are still called, every day, back to the life you used to live?

It's okay.

If you are struggling to welcome a new version of yourself after trauma, remember that healing is not a linear process. Progress might feel halting or uneven, and some days will be better than others. If you feel stuck, revisit the seven steps of the process in this book. *Different after You* is meant to be revisited as a guide for healing. As you reread, note which sections or what material seems the most challenging and focus on that. Perhaps you have more work to do to grieve the life, and the version of you, that you've lost. The process of rediscovering yourself is ongoing, with no finish line, and healing doesn't happen on a schedule.

It's okay to need more time.

Perhaps you are struggling or feeling pressured to heal more quickly? If you are in need of grace, use these statements to care for your healing self.

If you find yourself unable to love the version of you
born through trauma, offer yourself tenderness.
If you aren't able to release your daily heartache, offer
yourself consolation.

If you'd rather forget your traumatic experience than
relive one moment, offer yourself empathy.
If you can't stop yearning to return to the life you used
to live, offer yourself patience.
If you can't forgive yourself for what you view as failures — real or imagined — offer yourself mercy.
If you are so afraid of future heartbreak that you aren't
willing to take any risks, offer yourself kindness.
If you feel trapped by your trauma, offer yourself compassion.

After a traumatic experience, we all crave tenderness, consolation, empathy, patience, mercy, kindness, and compassion.
You have the power to offer or withhold these gifts for yourself.
What you most need to flourish is for *you* to honor your own
efforts — which includes whatever has been required to travel
this far. Give yourself acknowledgment, respect, compassion,
and dedication.

After years of thinking that my new self was less than the
person I used to be before Phil's death, I finally realized that
I wouldn't have survived if this "lesser" person had given up.
But she never did. She kept showing up, no matter how hard
the challenges were or how often I dismissed and belittled her
while I pined for the life I used to live. Step by painful step, this
self dragged me (often kicking and screaming) into the future
and built the life I live now.

As I worked to heal my heart, I began to understand the
value of who I was becoming. As I got more comfortable with
myself, I was less interested in fitting into my old skin, until
eventually I stopped wanting to. As I recognized the strength
and power I'd gained from my experiences, the more I wanted
to share with people how surviving Phil's death changed me.
When I was fully able to claim the version of me that was

shaped and refined by trauma, I began to confidently chart my own course.

Your future is in your hands, but don't worry. Today's version of you can be trusted to build a life of meaning, just for you.

The Birth of Your New Life

Years ago, I was at a Camp Widow event in San Diego milling around with hundreds of other widowed people on a gorgeous summer evening. After a full day of building community, we were relaxing and enjoying an outdoor reception when I was approached by a return camper who had discovered that painting was part of the new version of herself that emerged as she processed a combination of traumas in her life, including her husband's sudden death.

She was carrying a huge package as she walked toward me, but the smile on her face is what I remember most. This brave soul told me that she had a gift for me as she handed me the package. I pulled off the butcher paper from around a large canvas frame to reveal a stunning depiction of a brilliantly colored phoenix, the mythical bird who, according to Greek folklore, dies and is reborn in an unending cyclical pattern.

What struck me immediately was the boldness of both the image and the gift. Everything about this representation of a bird rising from the ashes of a prior self expresses power and courage. Rebirth isn't boring. The you who was born through this trauma can be bold and beautiful. There is no "less than" when a transcendent phoenix rises from the ashes of what came before.

This unique gift was also bold in how it represented this woman's owning of her new self — a self-taught painter offering me a piece of her earliest work in an effort to express not only her gratitude but her growth. Her courage was inspiring, and her work was a perfect expression of what happens when we claim our personal power after living through significant trauma.

Trauma survivors are the embodiment of the concept that rebirth can follow death. The experience that ends one version of our lives also gives birth to a new life. Owning our phoenix is a battle cry that screams, "This trauma did not kill me! This trauma made me who I am today! I choose to be proud of who I am and what I have become." Boldness, power, beauty, courage — these can all be the gifts of regeneration; the gifts that come from rising out of the ashes of what was and becoming what is.

Surviving a life-altering experience is an accomplishment. Full stop.

You did it. You lived. You are still standing.

Your presence in this moment confirms your survival, even if the life you are living right now is not what you consider your best life. Being on the other side of something awful is worth acknowledging and honoring. You have made it this far.

Experiencing trauma is not something anyone chooses, but we do have a choice about how we will live with what has happened. The direction your future takes is yours to determine. There will be times when the responsibility to shape your post-trauma life will feel heavy. Other times this freedom to choose will be exhilarating. As you design a life that reflects your current values, needs, and wishes, lean into every feeling that frightens you as well as those that uplift you. We need both grounding and lifting to thrive. When you choose to embody your new self and own the power that has been created by your survival, you may find that your soul can't help but sing.

In the time since I founded Soaring Spirits International, friends and strangers alike have assigned purpose to Phil's death by pointing to the transformation I experienced in the aftermath. Well-meaning people have assured me that Phil's death was not in vain because I was able to turn my tragedy into something positive. The prevailing message is that the good that resulted from Phil's accident makes his death okay.

No. No — all of this good does not make Phil's death okay.

Making meaning out of suffering doesn't give trauma value; it gives life value. Your life. And if the world is fortunate, your courage may also make the world a better place. Not because you suffered, but because you allowed that suffering to remake you.

Each time we integrate a new experience into our lives, we will be introduced to something new about the self who is evolving through trauma. There will be nuances to discover as we get to know the version of ourselves born through this challenge. As we practice allowing our past to inform our present and influence our future, we will be introduced again and again to new versions of ourselves. One self folds into the next, over and over again, throughout our lives.

The texture of our lives is created through the experiences we live and the discoveries we make along the way. Just like fashion, some fads will return in future iterations — so hang on to your bell-bottoms.

The things we release may come back to us in another form. Dreams, goals, preferences, and priorities may all shift if we are willing to continue to take inventory of our lives and ensure our priorities are still in line with our current values.

Eventually, another trauma will enter our lives and require us to dig into our past to access the tools we've collected in order to survive another tragedy. When that day comes, the process of rediscovery begins again.

Each time, we know more than we did before. Each time, we will recognize that we hold the key to moving through the traumatic experiences that alter our lives. Each time, we can lean on our past to help us not only survive whatever the present holds but also shape a future that matters. Integration gives us that power. Each time, we understand that trauma will change us, but those changes won't have the ability to determine the quality of our life.

Our continuous work is to willingly embrace ourselves as we evolve.

As you do, speak with the voice you found after living for a time without words. Feel with the heart you thought was irreparably shattered. Embody the version of yourself who didn't give up on you and carried you through every challenge that led you here. Walk around in this new skin and enjoy the sparkle! Preen, prance, and parade with pride as you step out as your new self. Allow people to know this you. Own the changes that have created the person you are today. Be unapologetically yourself, trusting in the value of what you know and who you've become.

You have only to choose. Then act. Then hold on — and keep holding until the holding on isn't hard anymore. That statement may sound simple, but simple and easy are not the same thing. The work of healing from and integrating trauma is never easy, though the goal is simple: to accept a life-altering experience, to embrace the changes that result, and to fully embody the new life we build from the ashes.

Claim that power, step into your new self, and let the world see you rise.

Afterword

I set out to pen this book fifteen years ago. While I feel some level of shock to have actually done it, there is one person who isn't surprised at all, my dad.

I entered Dan Neff's life when he was twenty — I was a surprise.

Every memory I have of my dad is of him supporting me and my goals. During elementary school, he built floats on which my whole family rode during the Troth Street school fall parade. Over the years, he created a variety of stages and props for musical theater performances, directed by my mom, and held in our front yard. My dad stood tall at countless school plays and award ceremonies so that I would know he was there.

When I was in high school, my cheerleading team was tasked with creating our own wooden boxes to provide an elevated platform for our cheers. When several of my teammates said they didn't have anyone to help them build their boxes, my dad handcrafted stadium-size wooden boxes for my entire cheerleading squad.

Three times he has walked me down the aisle with pride to my groom's side — celebrating each union with joy. When Phil died, he offered to build me and the kids a house behind the one he shares with my mom. When he made this offer, he said, "I just want to take care of you, Sweetie."

Dan Neff has always believed in his children and bragged about us at every opportunity. Achievement of stated goals isn't considered critical. What matters to my dad is whatever matters to us. His pride has never specifically been about the completion of the goal, but in the valiance of the effort.

When I called him to ask his opinion about whether I should attempt to write a book while running an international organization, he said, "Sweetie, the question isn't whether you *can* write a book; the question is whether you *will* write a book. You can do anything that you set your mind to."

The original idea for this book came to me just four months after Phil's death. I was desperate to figure out how to be widowed, and I thought other widows might have the answers to the million questions swirling in my brain. For one year I traveled the United States on weekends, showing up at the door of any widowed person willing to talk to me. I managed to interview thirty widows about their grief experiences, racking up ridiculous and hilarious travel stories along the way. My original plan was to use those interviews as the foundation for the book I would write. At every step of my yearlong quest, my dad offered support and confirmed his confidence in me.

About the time I completed my research, I decided that I would restore my maiden name by pairing it with Phil's last name, creating the mouthful that is Michele Neff Hernandez. I didn't care about the length of my name. I wanted to be known by the names that created the person I am today, and for my dad to see our family name on the cover of any book I might publish.

Though I had no experience writing a book proposal or finding an agent, I somehow succeeded at both, only to be crushed when no one in the publishing world showed any interest in my book. However, my dad was undaunted. He thought those publishers were crazy. He remained sure that our name would be on the cover of a book someday.

My dad also supported my efforts to create a community for widows, which led to Camp Widow and Soaring Spirits. He and my mom volunteered at the first several Camp Widow weekends, and for years they volunteered on 5K courses at our events. My dad built props for my keynote addresses, and he sat in the front row every time I was on a stage speaking — usually turning to the widowed people next to him and proudly informing them that "the lady up there" was his daughter.

Then, in 2018, my dad was diagnosed with lymphoma. Seven months of treatment were followed by a miraculous remission, allowing him to celebrate with my mom their fiftieth wedding anniversary. However, his health declined steadily afterward, and by November of 2020 the time came to stop treating his many ailments and choose the comfort of hospice care.

In the meantime, I had continued to seek a publisher for my book idea, and when I received the email that New World Library had accepted it, I was sitting next to my dad as he labored to breathe. I read him the email out loud as he alternated between telling me how proud he was of me and drifting off to sleep.

I've never taken care of a dying person. Phil's life ended in a moment, and his death experience did not include the day-to-day roller coaster that I've come to learn is part of dying one day at a time. Yet every painful part of my past experience with grief has provided me with skills that have supported my parents and my family as we say goodbye to the man whose love and support has shaped us.

I rely heavily on the skills I used to survive and thrive after Phil's death. Working with grieving people has made me very comfortable with the language around death. I don't shrink from hard truths. I am open to difficult conversations about the end of life. This is all knowledge that I have gained through trauma. The person I was before Phil died didn't have these skills, and she wouldn't have had the confidence that I do now to walk with my family through this time.

That said, neither the knowledge I've accumulated nor the skill set I've developed makes the fact that my dad is dying any easier.

That's another lesson from my past. Grief must be experienced; nothing can prepare you for the moment when a loved one dies. My father is still alive, but I know a new grief is coming, and I will have to evolve through another life-altering event.

The gift of integration is that I don't fear the evolution that is ahead, despite my familiarity with the pain accompanying earthly goodbyes. I can't imagine a life without my dad, and frankly, I don't want to. What I also know is that he lives within all the iterations of me. The lessons he has taught me, the way he has loved me, the joy that is so evident in him when I meet a personal goal — that all will continue to live inside. Even when my dad is no longer part of my present, through integration I can make space for my dad to be part of my life forever.

In the meantime, I am focused on right now. My dad is alive, planning to try out a new mermaid haircut (low and tight on the sides and long on top, which is totally in with the hip crowd) and to participate in a falconry experience, checking an item off his bucket list as a hawk flies off his arm. I am reveling in the moment, since the day will soon come when I will wish that I could update him on how my book is doing and what the kids are up to, and let him know how much the family he loves so much misses him.

This one is for you, Dad. I will always be different after you.

Acknowledgments

Different after You has been a labor of love fifteen years in the making. Through all of those years, I've been fortunate to be supported by several groups of people who make up my big, diverse, awesome global family. They have loved every version of me, and I've been shaped by sharing my life with them.

I am so grateful for my *Different after You* family. This book would likely still be a distant goal were it not for the amazing Kristine Carlson, who assured me that it was possible to write a book by committing to one hour of writing per day. Her support and the Book Doulas program changed my distant goal into a reality! Kris, thank you for inspiring me, challenging me, and leading the way with grace and generosity. Debra Evans, I feel like you are the other half of my brain and my heart. Your generosity of spirit paired with your intuitive and insightful talent have been an ongoing gift to me. Thank you for so lovingly and artfully shaping this work. You two are an incredible duo.

To my amazing agent, Stephanie Tade, and my friend Gretchen Van Nuys, thank you for believing in the power of integration and welcoming me into the Stephanie Tade Agency fold.

Thank you to my New World Library family. I am so grateful to Georgia Hughes, Marc Allen, Jeff Campbell, Kristen Cashman, Monique Muhlenkamp, Munro Magruder, and the rest of the team for their support, encouragement, and expertise as we moved this book from the notes on my desktop into a manuscript that could be delivered into the hands and hearts of my readers. I cannot imagine a better publishing home.

My Soaring Spirits family has shaped this book in so many ways. My widowed tribe has believed in this work from the very start. You've shared your stories with me, trusted me with your hearts and your loved ones, and generously shared the questions and challenges that widowhood has brought into your lives. This book would not be possible without you. Every single one of the widowed people I've met is reflected in these pages. You are incredible, and I am so honored to know you.

Stacey, thank you for so trustingly asking me the question that led to the development of the process that would become *Different after You*. Susan, thank you for gifting me with the perfect expression of rising from the ashes.

Sincere thanks to my first widowed family. Connie, Damaris, Karen, Shawna, Amy, Lisa, Michelle, Vera, Margaret, Mary, Shelley, Linda, Belinda, Mickie, Suzanne, Linda, Lisa, Toni, Juanita, Paula, Diane, Trish, Kimberly, and Joni: The experiences you shared with me so generously are the foundation for everything I've done since the year I spent connecting with all of you. Thank you for changing the world through your willingness to offer comfort to a young widow trying to find her way in an unknown world.

To the friends who have become family. Michelle, you changed my life (and so many others!) by your willingness to share yours with me. Thank you for walking every step of this road by my side and always reminding me to sing in the lifeboat. Kath, you've helped to shape my heart, my life, this book, and my understanding of the universe. Dana, your belief in me and your support of all of my crazy ideas has made so many of them realities. Thank you for believing in me. Terry, your enthusiasm and support have been a gift, time and time again. I am so grateful to have walked this road with you. My Soaring Spirits team, large and small, your support and encouragement has meant the world to me. Thank you all for sticking with me through thick and thin! To my tribe of fifty — Michelle, Lisa, Kim, and Carrie: thank you for being the kind of women who lift one another up with support, laughter, and memes! Gail and Ron ... I finally did it! Thank you for believing in me and encouraging my growth, step by step. To my incredible group of friends who have stood beside me through every one of the steps outlined in this process, there will never be enough words of gratitude. Finally, a shout-out to each of my friends who are published authors and who shared their experiences, their encouragement, their expertise, and even their agents with me. You have set an inspiring example, and I am so honored to join your ranks.

My big, loud, wild Neff family. The foundation of the community I've built was fostered by your example and your love. You have held me up, wiped my tears, celebrated my joys, and encouraged my dreams. Thank you, Mom and Dad, for every lesson you've taught me, especially the ones about compassion, kindness, and the value of unconditional love.

Michael, Denise, David, Danielle, Debi, and Danny: Thank you for loving and supporting every version of me, and for always having my back. You are all the best gift Mom and Dad ever gave me.

Dan, Drea, Jake, and Dan: Your support and love are appreciated more than you know.

Izaak, Andrew, Ethan, Eveline, Lyra, David, Vincent, Abigail, Elijah, Miles, and Wesley: I could not be more proud of you, and I can't wait to see how the world is changed by your brilliance.

Deepest thanks and love to my little Dare-Hernandez-Ibanez-Marrin-Castro-Dias family. Michael, thank you for loving me so generously, being my biggest fan, and consistently being my soft place to land. Caitlin, John, and Josh, thank you for expanding my mind, my heart, and my understanding of the world. Becoming your mother changed my life in the best possible way. Joaquin, Sedona, and Andrea, thank you for expanding our family with such beautiful love.

Thank you to my Australian family for welcoming a girl from across the world into your hearts.

Last but never least to my love Phillip Hernandez. Lipe, through every iteration of my life, I will love you still.

About the Author

Michele Neff Hernandez was widowed at thirty-five when her husband Phillip was killed in a cycling accident in 2005. Finding herself struggling through unknown emotional territory, she set out to find other widowed people and to ask them a set of fifty practical questions. What she discovered over one year of interviewing widowed people across the United States fueled the creation of Soaring Spirits International, an inclusive, secular, nonprofit organization whose mission is to foster resilience and support grief recovery in the widowed population.

Michele is a content expert and speaker in the areas of resilience, bereavement, adapting to life challenges, nonprofit leadership, and women's issues. She is the creator and director of the innovative Camp Widow program. Michele has worked with the families of fallen firefighters, the widowed spouses of members of Special Operations units, surviving spouses of Covid-19 patients, and widowed people from all walks of life.

She has won numerous national and local awards for her work with grieving populations and was named a 2021 CNN Hero.

Michele is the CEO of Soaring Spirits International and the executive director of Soaring Spirits Canada. She also acts as the director of the Soaring Spirits Resilience Center located in Kerrville, Texas, whose mission is to research resilience and create practical tools for building resilience in the bereaved.

Michele's grief experience has expanded her heart and increased the love she has for her awesome kids, her huge, wild family, her incredible tribe of friends, and her kindhearted Aussie husband. To connect with Michele, visit her website at micheleneffhernandez.com.

About Soaring Spirits International

Soaring Spirits International

Soaring Spirits International (soaringspirits.org) is an inclusive, secular, nonprofit organization that offers innovative, life-affirming events, groups, and online programs for any person who has outlived a spouse or partner. Founded in May 2008, Soaring Spirits has uplifted, inspired, and sustained millions of widowed people, and it has since branched out to include Soaring Spirits Canada.

Camp Widow

Camp Widow (campwidow.org) is Soaring Spirits' flagship program. It offers one-day and weekend-long events designed to foster resilience, enhance positive coping skills, and build community for widowed people of all ages, genders, nationalities, orientations, and backgrounds. Camp Widow is a unique blend of conference, retreat, and getaway that assists widowed people in rebuilding their lives post-loss by offering workshops, presentations, and healing in a community atmosphere that promotes hope for the future.

Soaring Spirits Resilience Center

Founded in 2017, the Soaring Spirits Resilience Center (widowedresilience.org) is located at Schreiner University in Kerrville, Texas. The center's purpose is to collect resilience-related data and to use that research to craft practical tools and relevant programming designed specifically to foster confidence and hope for people who've experienced the death of their life partner. In essence, the center's work focuses on helping people suffering from trauma to focus their limited energy in ways that foster personal growth and increased life satisfaction.

Research shows that integration is one of the major indicators of increased resilience, healthy coping, and the development of grit and optimism in widowed people, and the center is developing assessment tools that refine the definition of resilience as it relates to widowhood. The first tool that's been developed is the Soaring Spirits Widowhood Resilience Scale (the research was published in the *OMEGA Journal of Death and Dying*, September 11, 2019). This self-assessment tool measures resilience using everyday factors like the ability to laugh regularly and the ability to foster a supportive community as markers for measuring healing from the trauma and grief related to the death of a loved one.

NEW WORLD LIBRARY is dedicated to publishing books and other media that inspire and challenge us to improve the quality of our lives and the world.

We are a socially and environmentally aware company. We recognize that we have an ethical responsibility to our readers, our authors, our staff members, and our planet.

We serve our readers by creating the finest publications possible on personal growth, creativity, spirituality, wellness, and other areas of emerging importance. We serve our authors by working with them to produce and promote quality books that reach a wide audience. We serve New World Library employees with generous benefits, significant profit sharing, and constant encouragement to pursue their most expansive dreams.

Whenever possible, we print our books with soy-based ink on 100 percent postconsumer-waste recycled paper. We power our offices with solar energy and contribute to nonprofit organizations working to make the world a better place for us all.

Our products are available wherever books are sold. Visit our website to download our catalog, subscribe to our e-newsletter, read our blog, and link to authors' websites, videos, and podcasts.

customerservice@newworldlibrary.com
Phone: 415-884-2100 or 800-972-6657
Orders: Ext. 110 • Catalog requests: Ext. 110
Fax: 415-884-2199

www.newworldlibrary.com